THE GREATEST BOOK of POLITICAL CARTOONS ON THE TRUMP PRESIDENCY WITH A FLASHBACK TO THE DEMOCRAT & REPUBLICAN CANDIDATES OF 2016

Richard Friedman

President Donald Trump pumping his Fist After Addressing the crowd during his swearing-in-ceremony on JANUARY 20 At the Capitol in Washington, D.C.

CONTENTS

Introduction I

I
<u>INTRODUCTION</u>

"If humanity cannot live with the dangers and responsibilities inherent in freedom, it will probably turn to authoritarianism."

The above quote is from the Germany born author of the book "Escape From Freedom" (1942). In his book which was written after Hitler had come to power, Erich Fromm raises the question of whether or not democracy such as that found outside of Germany makes a people safe from similar developments.

The three chapters of political cartoons comprising this book take the reader on an informative, humorous, and at times hysterical journey. It begins with Chapter I, Up To Date On the Donald J. Trump Presidency (2018), followed with Chapter II, The First Year (2017), and concluding with Chapter III, The Baking of President Trump's Victory of 2016. This final chapter is divided into banter between the major Democrat & Republican candidates for their party's presidential nomination.

Whether or not Erich Fromm's above quote is relevant in today's world is also at the center of this book, and what further impelled me to create it.

Richard Friedman

1. Up To Date On The Donald J. Trump
   Presidency (2018)

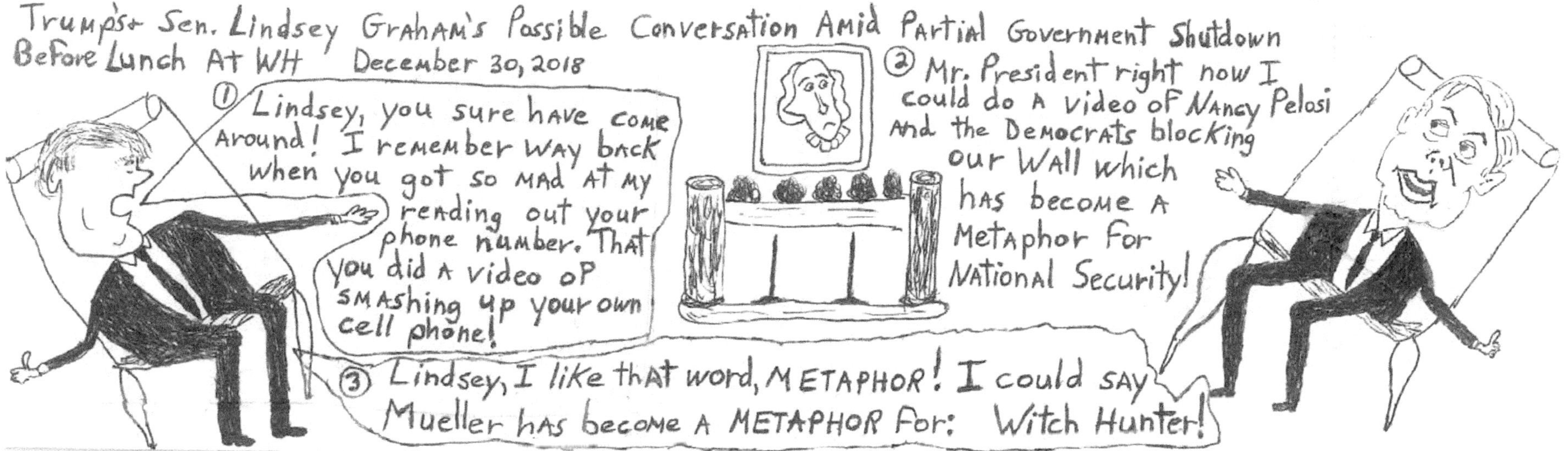

Trump's & Sen. Lindsey Graham's Possible Conversation Amid Partial Government Shutdown Before Lunch At WH   December 30, 2018
① Lindsey, you sure have come around! I remember way back when you got so mad at my reading out your phone number. That you did a video of smashing up your own cell phone!
② Mr. President right now I could do a video of Nancy Pelosi and the Democrats blocking our Wall which has become a Metaphor for National Security!
③ Lindsey, I like that word, METAPHOR! I could say Mueller has become a METAPHOR for: Witch Hunter!

Trump's Pre-Election 2020 Market Meltdown Nightmare Featuring His Treasury Secretary Steven Mnuchin & Federal Reserve Chairman Jerome Powell

The Apparent Trump Doctrine of Today Compared To The Truman Doctrine That Became Foundation of American Foreign Policy Till Now...

The Truman Doctrine to Counter Soviet geopolitical expansion during The Cold War: March 12, 1947

The Trump Doctrine On A surprise visit to Iraq talking to U.S. Troops on leaving Syria: December 26, 2018

Trump Has Lashed Out At His Hand-Picked Acting Attorney General Matt Whitaker For Failing To Do More To Control the Manhattan U.S. Attorney's Office And Its Prosecution of Michael Cohen, According To CNN: How A WH Meeting Might Have Went... December 22, 2018
① Look Matt, for all I care you can crucify Cohen. But as my selected Attorney General you are supposed to protect me from being implicated!
③ Obstruction of what Justice! There's no justice with collusion. And there's NO COLLUSION!
② Mr. President, if I interfere with the Mueller investigation on your behalf I could face charges of Obstruction of JUSTICE!

Trump's Defense Secretary, Jim Mattis According To WH Official Before Resigning Made Last Ditch Effort At The White House To Talk The President Out Of His Decision To Withdraw The U.S. From Syria: How It Might Have Gone...

Dec. 20, 2018

Trump's Decision To Reverse Himself On Backing Off His Demand For Money For A Border Wall With With Mexico That Would Have Kept Government Running Until February 8 Is Pararalled With Conservative Media Talk Show Host Rush Limbaugh's Meteoric Rise Of Influence In Trump World

The Nightmare That Drove Trump To Wish Michael Flynn "Good Luck" Hours Before He Was To Be Sentenced In Federal Court For Lying To The FBI December 18, 2018

Trump Announces The Resignation of Ryan Zinke In Below Tweet Amid Multiple Investigations...Dec. 15, 2018 And His Noteworthy Accomplishments Coupled With His Outdoor Marlboro Man IMAGE

Donald J. Trump ✓
@realDonaldTrump

Secretary of the Interior@ Ryan Zinke will be leaving the Administration At the end of the Year AFter having served For A period of Almost two years. Ryan has Accomplished much during his tenure And I want to thank him For his service to our Nation......

9:14 AM - Dec. 15, 2018

<u>Some of Zinke's Greatest Accomplishments</u>
① His Agency had taken steps to open the door to oil exploration in Alaska's Arctic National Wildlife Refuge.
② He had Announced plans to repeal An important Fracking safety rule, And loosen... safety guidelines for underwater drilling.
③ He had Announced that entrance fees for some of America's most popular national parks will increase substantially.

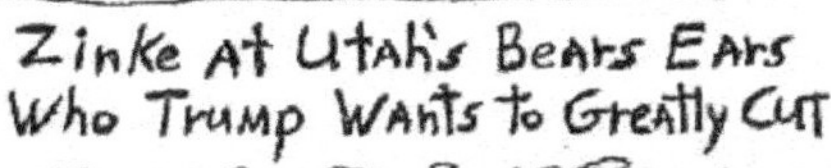

Zinke At Utah's Bears Ears Who Trump Wants to Greatly CUT

Trump's Possible Job Interview With His Budget Director Mick Mulvaney Before Selecting Mulvaney To Replace John Kelly As White House Chief of Staff   Dec. 14, 2018
② Mr. President, you have to understand I don't want to be your next White House Chief of Staff!
① Mick... I bet you think you are here for our scheduled meeting to discuss the federal budget!
③ Fantastic! Then you will act like you are. You will be Acting White House Chief of Staff!

Rudy Giuliani, Trump's Attorney Says Trump's Alleged Campaign Finance Violations Are Fine Because "Nobody Got Killed" Basically Saying...

December 14, 2018

Trump's Gone With The Money And Back With The Wind Stormy Daniels Story-
And What He Might Have Been Thinking...

Trump's Jerry Mahoney & Mike Pompeo Puppet Show Given Pompeo Has Called CIA's Khashoggi Investigation Partly Inaccurate & Incomplete
1 Mr. President, how COME that Mikey dummy has NO STRINGS Like Me?
Dec. 13, 2018
2 Jerry... It's because you are a low IQ dummy And My Mikey here who is doing A FANTASTIC job as Secretary of State... has A very high IQ... Listen...
3 Mr. President, you Are right on! Saudi Arabia is an important Ally of the U.S. And the Killing of U.S. based journalist Jamal Khashoggi is still being investigated. And We can't comment on whether we believe the denials From the Crown Prince!

Trump Concerned About House Impeachment From WH Sources: Tweets During Nightmare

Trump Takes Pride In Threatening A Government Shutdown Over His Border Wall Funding In Oval Office Meeting With Top Democrat Leaders of House & Senate: His Possible After Thoughts...

Trump Ponders The Stepping Down of WH Chief of Staff John Kelly. And Leading Candidate For His Replacement Declining Trump's Offer   December 10, 2018

WANTED: WH CHIEF OF STAFF

① MUST BE ENTHUSIASTIC ABOUT FIRING PEOPLE

② MUST HAVE A POSITIVE ATTITUDE TOWARDS ADDING CHAOS

③ MUST BE LOYAL TO PRESIDENT [NO NAME-CALLING] 'TARIFF MAN' MAY BE ACCEPTABLE AT TIMES

④ MUST BE A SEEKER OF REAL TRUTH BY KEEPING PRESIDENT'S TWITTER Iphone FULLY CHARGED

Trump's Tweet Shortly After the Release of
Sentencing Memos For his Former Personal
Attorney, Michael Cohen. Who had Admitted
he Acted in coordination with And At the
direction of Individual-1 {Trump} In payments.

Donald J. Trump
@realDonaldTrump

December 7, 2018
6:00 PM

Totally clears the President Thank you!

Trump's possible vision As he tweeted
the Above →

Trump Lashes Out At His Former Secretary of State Rex Tillerson After Tillerson Says President Asked Him To Sidestep the Law... Trump's Tweet And Trump's Possible Afterthoughts
December 7, 2018

Donald J. Trump ✓
@realDonaldTrump

Mike Pompeo is doing a great job, I am very proud of him. His predecessor, Rex Tillerson, didn't have the mental capacity needed. He was dumb as a rock and I couldn't get rid of him fast enough. He was lazy as hell. Now it is a whole new ballgame, great spirit at State!

Trump's Possible Afterthought... Tillerson's ballgame was like this Abbott & Costello of – Who's On First?

Trump's Tweet Hours After Bush's Funeral Reminds Country of His Rasmussen Approval
Rating And Possible Afterthoughts   December 6, 2018

50%

APPROVAL RATING

PROMISES MADE	PROMISES KEPT

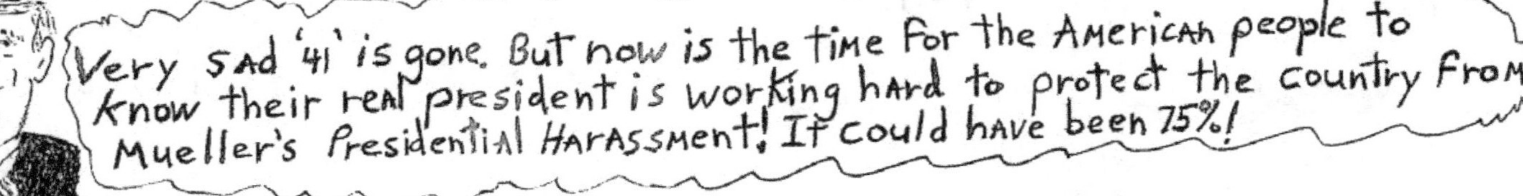

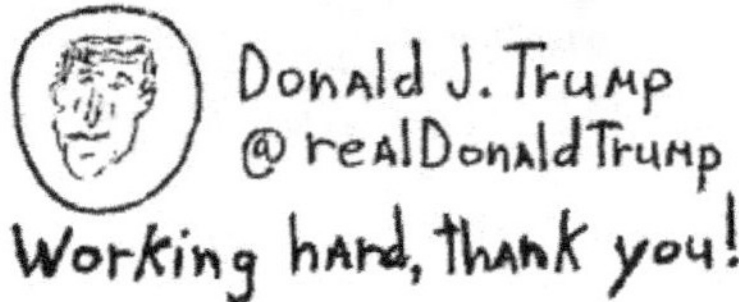

Donald J. Trump
@ realDonaldTrump

Working hard, thank you!

Trump Demands Stiff Prison Sentence For His Ex-Lawyer Michael Cohen, For Cohen's Admitted Crimes   December 3, 2018: And What he Refrained From Saying...?
I would include challenging work in a chain gang:

Donald J. Trump ✓
@realDonaldTrump

"Michael Cohen Asks judge For no Prison Time." You mean he can do all of the TERRIBLE, unrelated to Trump, things having to do with Fraud, big loans, Taxis, etc., and not serve a long prison term?

He lied for this outcome and should, in my opinion, serve a full and complete sentence.

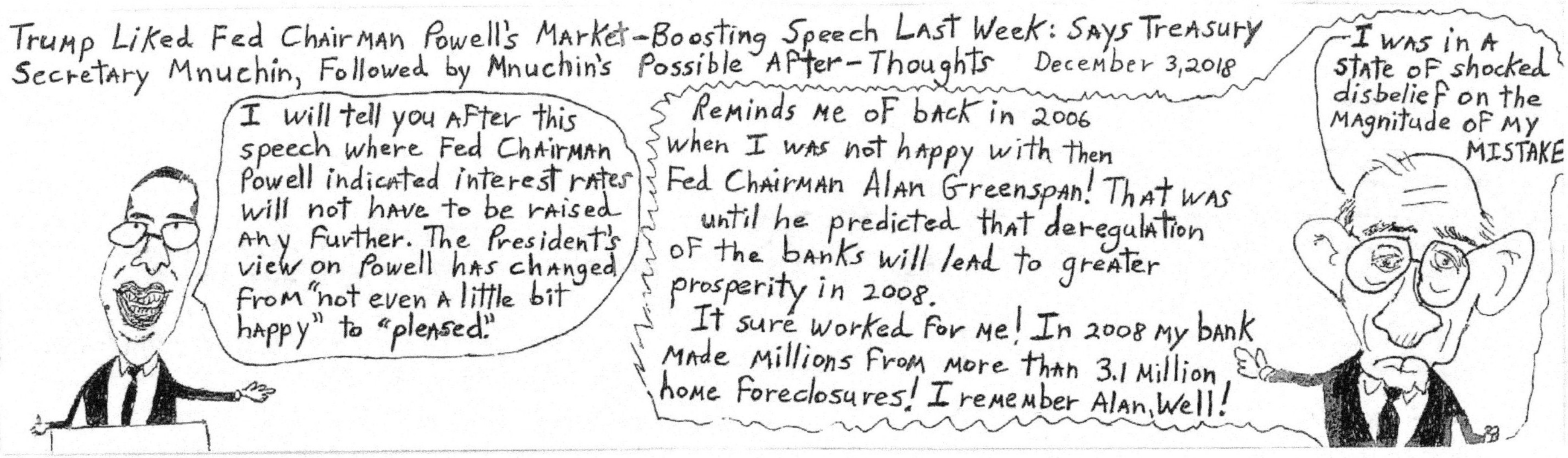

Trump Liked Fed Chairman Powell's Market-Boosting Speech Last Week: Says Treasury Secretary Mnuchin, Followed by Mnuchin's Possible After-Thoughts   December 3, 2018
I will tell you after this speech where Fed Chairman Powell indicated interest rates will not have to be raised any further. The President's view on Powell has changed from "not even a little bit happy" to "pleased."
Reminds me of back in 2006 when I was not happy with then Fed Chairman Alan Greenspan! That was until he predicted that deregulation of the banks will lead to greater prosperity in 2008.
It sure worked for me! In 2008 my bank made millions from more than 3.1 million home foreclosures! I remember Alan, well!
I was in a state of shocked disbelief on the magnitude of my MISTAKE

The Ghost of the Late Former President '41' George H.W. Bush Returns To The Oval Office
December 3, 2018
② Remember '41' there is A thing cAlled the U.S. SenAte where I hAve even more Republicans now!
① Mr. President, with due respect: You bullied yourself into the Presidency And now you Are bullying in the opposite direction!
③ Not After I stArt haunting Lindsey GrahAm + Mitch McConnell!

Trump's Possible Nightmare Triggered By Michael Cohen Admitting That he Lied to Congress About the Trump Organization's Business Aspirations In Moscow As Evidenced By Cohen's Admission of Meeting With Putin's Press Secretary During Presidential Campaign To Discuss the Proposed Trump Tower Moscow That Included Penthouse For Putin.
Nov. 30, 2018

Trump's Arrival At Buenos Aires, Argentina Airport TO Possibly One MARACAS PLAyer
Compared To China's Xi Jinping Welcomed With A Military Band For G20 Conference
Demonstrates Argentina's Will To Get Closer To China   Nov. 29, 2018

In Wake of Trump Submitted Answers To Written Questions On Russia & Paul Manafort Losing His Plea Deal Because Mueller Suspected He Told Big Lies: Mueller's Possible Administering Of Lie Detector Test To Paul Manafort...

Trump Says He Was "Very Tough" On GM's CEO Mary Barra Over Her Decision To Close Four Plants in the U.S. Because of Dropping Demand For Sedans: And Goes On to Single Out Ohio (TRUMP COUNTRY) Where Republicans Just Swept the Races For Governor And Four Other State Offices: And What Trump Didn't Say... November 26, 2018

Trump Attorney Giuliani Brags About Manafort-Trump Alliance Despite Manafort's Lawyer Continued to Brief Trump's Legal Team During His Plea-Deal Agreement With Mueller's Russia Investigation Team, November 28, 2018   And Given Joint Defense Agreements Are For People With Common Legal Interests...

WHAT HE SAID...

WHAT HE FORGOT TO SAY...

The two legal teams often played golf together At President Trump's National Doral Golf Course. There they had Further great discussions About Mueller's Russian Investigation.
All had A FANTASTIC time!

Below President Trump Basically Predicts the Coming of American Heroes Who Will NOT Be With Mueller... A Possible Heroe Below Has Refused A Plea Deal. According to Trump He Could Have Spoken In the Same Spirit of the American Patriot Nathan Hale On September 22, 1776...

Trump Has Dream About Acting Attorney General Whitaker Following Times Report That Trump's WH Counsel Wrote A Memo To Dissuade Trump From Using Justice Dept. To Prosecute Hillary Clinton & Ex-FBI Director James Comey November 21, 2018

Trump During California Visit Blames Its Forest Management For Wild Fires And Says California Should Take Lessons From Finland, A Country With 57 Million Acres Of Forests And Does Lots Of Raking According To Its President... As Trump Imagines   November 19, 2018

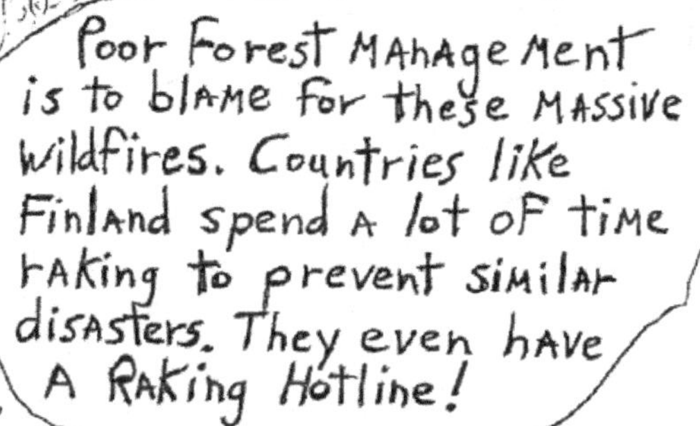

A TRUMP <u>FLASHFORWARD</u> To the Now Established WH Rule That Reporters At Press Conferences Can Be Banned by the President From Asking Follow-Up Questions- A Hypothetical Space Force & Company Budget Question...

November 26, 2018

A Possible Future Meeting Between Trump & Putin Nov. 30, 2018 AT Buenos Aires Summit Given Trump's PAST PerFormance And The Nov. 25, 2018 Incident oF Russia's CoAst Guard Firing On And Seizing Three UKrainian Vessels NeAr CrimeAn PeninsulA

Trump's Response AFter Supreme Court ChieF Justice John Roberts Rebuked the President SAying the U.S. Doesn't HAve "ObAmA Judges or Trump Judges, Bush Judges or Clinton Judges"

November 21, 2018

Trump Stands With Saudi Arabia And Defends Crown Prince Over Khashoggi Murder Contradicting CIA's Latest Findings And His Possible After-Thoughts
November 20, 2018

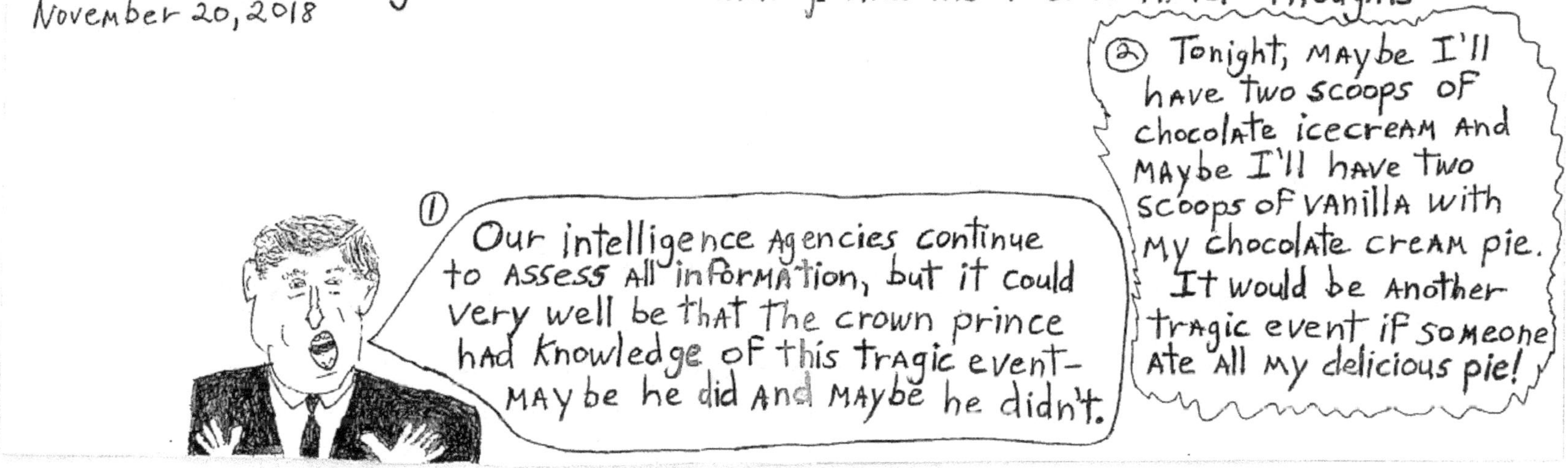

Trump Digs In On His Criticism Of the Hunt For Osama Bin Laden And Dispute With the Retired Admiral Who Oversaw U.S. Military Operation In Which Bin Laden WAS Killed

November 19, 2018

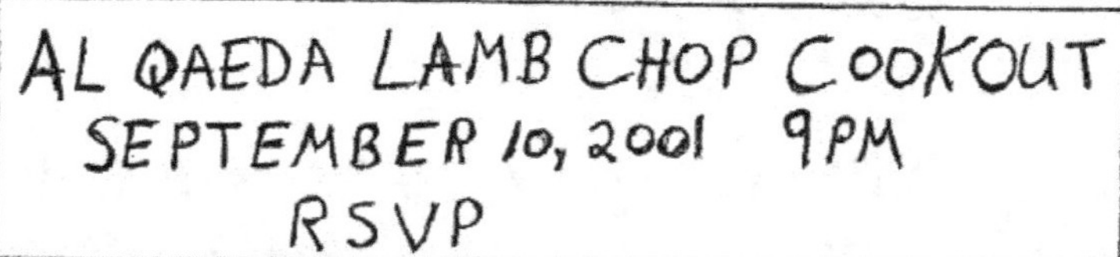

Trump's Dream of Delivering Graduation Speech Following Tweet: Universities Will someday study what highly conflicted (and NOT Senate Approved) Bob Mueller and his gang of Democrat thugs have done to destroy people
November 18, 2018
CLASS OF 2020
BARBECUE UNIVERSITY
PRESIDENT OF THE UNITED STATES
Class of 2020 it will serve you well to remember that what you read and what you hear is NOT happening. That incredible knowledge can make any of you a future president of the United States!

Trump's Possible Tutor He Forgot To Mention When He Said He Alone Answered A Set OF Questions From Special Counsel Mueller's TAKE Home Interview Test "VERY EASILY"

November 16, 2018

Trump's Decision To Deploy Thousands of Troops To The Border At Huge Expense To Prepare For The Arrival of Migrant Caravans Is Defended by Defense Secretary Mattis As He Compares The Arrival of Migrant Caravans To The 1916 Raid Into The U.S. Led By Gen. Francisco "Pancho" Villa From Mexico   November 15, 2018

A Possible Meeting Between Republican Sen. Lindsey Graham And Trump Appointed Acting Attorney General Matt Whitaker Following Graham Saying On "Face the Nation" Whitaker Doesn't Have To Recuse Himself In the Mueller Russia Probe: And Whitaker's Past Speculation That Another Attorney General Appointed By President Trump Could Just Cut Funds To Mueller Probe... November 15, 2018

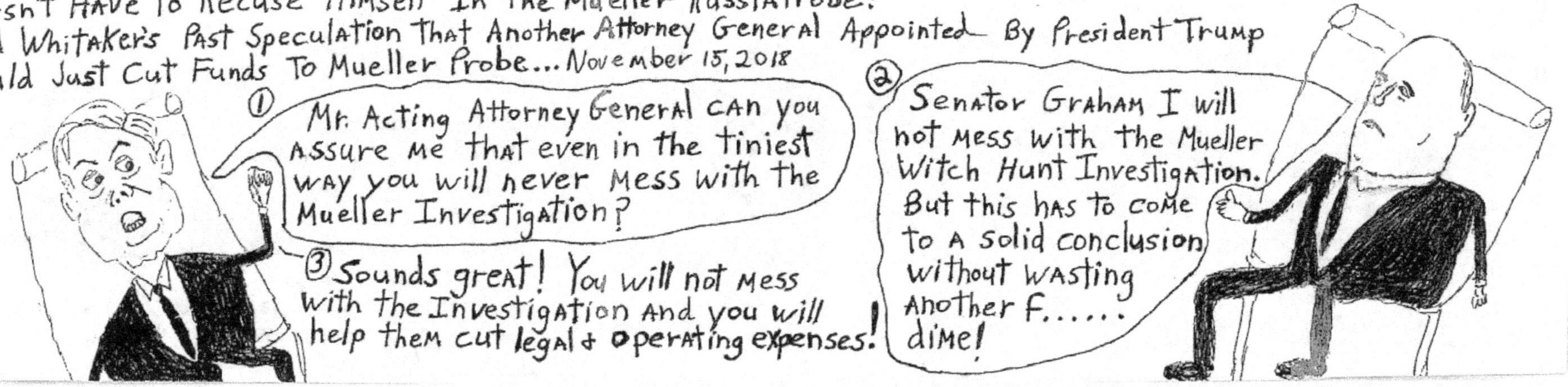

Trump's Post-Election News Conference On North Korea: __Facts:__ The Term Denuclear-ization In The Document Signed By Trump And North Korean Leader Could Be Viewed By Both Countries Very Differently. In May, North Korea Blew Up Tunnels And Called This Proof of its Commitment To End Nuclear Testing, But A Senior WH Official Accused Pyongyang Of Breaking A Promise To Allow Experts To Witness It. Below the Only Witness To What Actually Occurred...

November 14, 2018

Trump At Post-Election News Conference Optimizes Losing The House By Expounding On His CAMPAign Rallies And TAKes A Shot At The MediA—With Possible Response From Stephen Colbert November 7, 2018

A Future Press Conference In 2020 If The Trump Administration's Removal Of Jim Acosta's White House Press Pass Which Arguably Violates His Due Process Rights Guaranteed By The Fifth Amendment Is Permitted To Stand

Nov. 14, 2018

Trump's Secret Plan to Deploy Former V.P. Cheney When He Reversed His Claim that U.S.
Would Shoot Rock-Throwing Migrants   November 2, 2018

Trump Has Dream of Changing The Twenty - Second Amendment To Allow Him A Third Term Following His Posted Tweet Blaming Democrats For "Letting in" Luis Bracamontes, the man who killed two law enforcement officials in 2014   November 1, 2018

Trump's Pre-Election Theory That He Can End Birthright Citizenship Enacted In 1868 By The 14th Amendment   October 30, 2018

Newt Gingrich Says if Democrats Re-take Control of the House And Subpoena Trump's Tax Returns, It Would likely Force A Fight in the Supreme Court   October 26, 2018

Trump Says Pittsburgh Synagogue Should Have Had Armed Guards - October 28, 2018
Trump's Vision of A Safe Bar Mitzvah
IF there WAS An Armed guard inside the temple, they would have been Able to stop him...

Trump, According to the New York Times At Times Uses An Unsecured Personal iPhone To Contact Friends That Has Resulted In The Chinese Eavesdropping On His Conversations — How telephone chat with friend, Sean Hannity On pig Farmers Feeling the pinch From Trump's Tariffs Might have gone... October 26, 2018

Trump Has A Fantastic Dream of A Photo of Democrat House Minority Leader Nancy Pelosi Buying A Rolls-Royce For A Migrant After FBI Unable to Find Photos of Comey, Mueller "hugging And Kissing" As Trump Claimed.   October 24, 2018

Trump Tries Bipartisanship After Bombs Sent To Prominent Critics of Himself,
Failed To Detonate October 24, 2018

Trump Has Fantastic Dream of Body-Slamming CNN Reporter Wolf Blitzer Following the President Calling A Republican Congressman Who Body-Slammed A Reporter "My Guy"
October 20, 2018

The Least Admired Presidents In U.S. History Come Back To Give Thanks To President Trump.

October 20, 2018

Trump Tells Reporters He Is Not Aware Of The Loud & Riveting Clash Between His White House Chief Of STAFF, John Kelly And NAtional Security Adviser John Bolton Outside His OvAl OFFice BeFore BoArding Air Force One to Travel To Montana Campaign Rally Oct.18,2018

Trump's Nightmare After the President Complained About Rising Interest Rates, Calling the U.S. Federal Reserve "My Biggest Threat" — Trump Owes Deutsche Bank AG About $340 Million with interest rates that will rise when the Fed raises interest rates on loans that are <u>not</u> at a Fixed rate Oct. 16, 2018

Trump Says Saudi King Strongly Denies Involvement In Khashoggi Disappearance Later Telling His Own Possible Theory That "rogue Killers" Could Have Been Responsible   October 15, 2018
Consulate of Saudia Arabia - Istanbul
I don't want to get into the King's Mind! He strongly denies it! But to Me it sounds like it could be rogue Killers!
Rogue Killers Convention WELCOME! Conference 2 PM Exhibition 4 PM

Trump's Likely Thoughts After Defense Secretary James Mattis Said "he never registered for Any political party" Following Trump Calling Him "sort of A Democrat" on A "60 Minutes" Interview   October 15, 2018

Democrat Tillerson   Democrat Mattis

Trump's Fantastic Dream Of Honoring Rep. Devin Nunez Following His Statement That the House Representative Should Get the Medal oF Honor For His Support oF the President And For Handling oF Russia Probe. Oct. 11, 2018

This man's midnight run dash to the White House in the dark & cold night oF March 21, 2018 to review reports About Obama Tapping my phones beFore the 2016 election will go down in history with the Midnight Ride oF Paul Revere!

Trump Raises Possibility Replacing Attorney General Jeff Sessions With Sessions Own chief-of-staff
& Former Football Player
Trump Loyalist Matthew
Whitaker
Oct. 10, 2018
TRUMP 2020
I still want my Disneyworld ticket Trump promised me on Air Force One coming back from Orlando!

Trump Possible Meeting With Secretary of State Mike Pompeo Following His Meeting With
North Korean Leader Kim Jong Un On
October 7, 2018

Trump Turns W.H. Swearing-In For Supreme Court Justice Brett Kavanaugh Into Political Pep Rally As Justice Ruth Bader Ginsburg Shows Her True Sentiments— Trump's Inner Thoughts Possible... Oct. 8, 2018

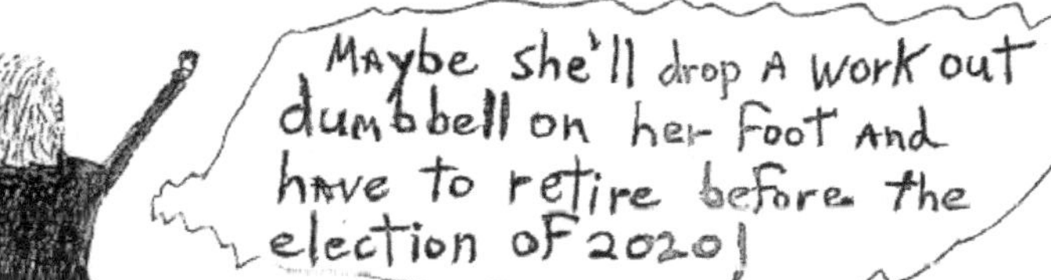

Trump Apologizes To Now Supreme Court Justice Brett Kavanaugh At Swearing - In Event At The White House Oct. 8, 2018 Coupled With His "Historic Scrutiny"

The Historic Scrutiny of Brett Kavanaugh's Personal Handwritten Calendar From 1982 He Submitted — On July 1, 1982 he attended a beer party of a gathering of 7 boys with his friend, Squi at Timmy's house. And nobody else remembers any other party like Dr. Ford described in her allegations on that day and time...

Chuck Grassley's Tweet Oct. 4, 2018 Coupled With A Possible Symbolic Scenario OF How The FBI Was Constrained In Their Investigation oF Judge Brett Kavanaugh's Fitness For the Supreme Court

Chuck Grassley ✓ @ChuckGrassley

Supplemental FBI background File For Judge Kavanaugh has been received by @senjudiciary Ranking Member Feinstein & I have Agreed to Alternating *EQUAL* Access For senators to study content From Additional background info gathered by non-partisan FBI Agents...

Trump's Kavanaugh Nightmare After the President Said "I watched him and I was surprised at how vocal he was about the fact that he likes beer" And Kavanaugh being possibly Confirmed by Senate Oct.1, 2018
SUPREMA CORTE
This Bud's For You President TRUMP!

President Trump Exerts His Enthusiasm For His Detente with North Korean Leader Kim Jong Un By Declaring At A Rally With Supporters that "We Fell in love" After Exchanging Letters Plus His Though[t]

September 29, 2018

PROMISES KEPT

② If we break up! This will be the GREATEST LOVERS QUARREL in the history of the WORLD!

① I WAS really tough And so was he. And we went back And Forth. And then we fell in love, OK? No, really, he wrote me beautiful letters, And they're great letters. We fell in love.

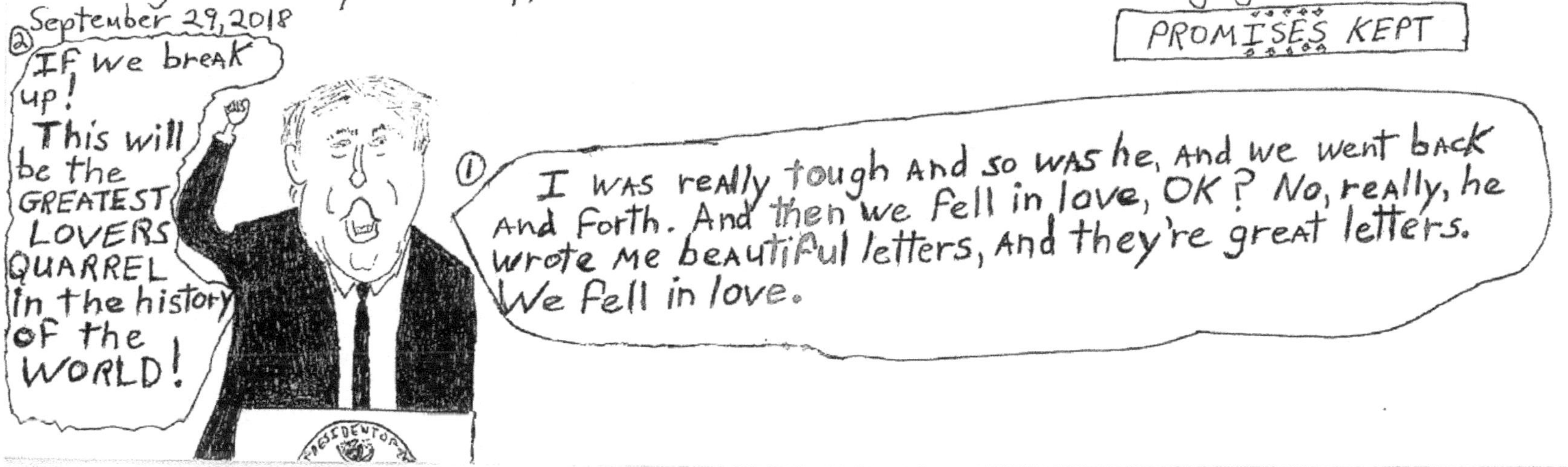

Sen. Lindsey Graham's BLAST In DeFense oF Trump's Supreme Court Nominee Brett Kavanaugh At The Hearing — His Attack on Democrats He Now Defends

September 29, 2018

The Rise of Lindsey Graham And the Fall of Jeff Sessions In TRUMP WORLD September 27, 2018
1
—The problems between the president & Sessions go beyond Sessions' recusal From Mueller's Russia probe. The Dept. of Justice needs A voice the White House people will listen to!
3
—Heil TRUMP!
2
—This KAVANAugh hearing is An unethical shAm!
Bye TRUMP!
4

Trump Addresses New Kavanaugh Claims in Press Conference And Alludes To A
Democrat Laughing Room In Capitol
September 26, 2018

President Trump's Opening Statement On Occasion of Addressing UN General Assembly: Appearing like An Election Speech & His Possible Thoughts As Laughter Erupted...
September 25, 2018

① In less than two years my Administration has accomplished more than almost any other Administration in the history of my country.

② Laughter

③ I didn't expect that.

IF I'M ever impeached I can now get my own TRUMP TONIGHT SHOW!

PRESIDENT UNITED STATES

Trump & Chuck Grassley, Chairman of the Senate Judiciary Committee Lead Republicans off Kavanaugh Cliff to support the Judge who wrote presidents shouldn't be "distracted" by Criminal Investigations   Sept. 25, 2018.
— March over that cliff! In the name of TRUMP!
— You must march over that cliff to stop the Democrats who are running a Con Game!
Kavanaugh
Kavanaugh Cliff
Kavanaugh
Kavanaugh
Kavanaugh

VP Mike Pence Has Trump 25th Amendment Impeachment Nightmare After New York Times Reports Deputy Attorney General Rod Rosenstein Proposed Recruiting Cabinet Members & Wearing A Wire to Record his Interactions With Trump

Sept. 24, 2018

Deputy Attorney General Expecting to be Fired Meets With W.H. Chief of Staff John Kelly: How it Might Have Gone   Sept. 24, 2018
ROD
① Mr. Rosenstein the President does not like to Fire people like on The Apprentice! IF you would resign you would Avoid the Attorney General Sessions DOG HOUSE TREATMENT!
② I AM prepared for the treatment! My new HOUSE!

Trump's Supreme Court Pick Kavanaugh Is Lie Detector Nightmare After His Accuser of Sexual Assault, Christine Blasey Ford Passes Her Test!
Sept. 20, 2018

Trump's Michael Cohen Nightmare After Cohen "Alleges that he was present, along with several others when Trump was informed of the Russians' offer by Trump Jr. to meet with the Russians." And Cohen when interviewed by ABC said of his loyalties: "I put family and country first."   Sept. 21, 2018

Trump Launches New Attack On Jeff Sessions Saying His Response & Thoughts On W.H Lawn When Asked →
"I don't have an Attorney general. It's very sad. Are you going to fire the Attorney General?
Sept. 19, 2018
We are looking at lots of different things!

Trump Orders Documents Relative to Russia Investigation Declassified From being Secret. As Democrats speak Out that it Endangers National Security and Republicans Appear to Believe Transparency Should be the "Most Important Consideration! Sept. 17, 2018

Sept. 14, 2018
Giuliani's Evolution On Manafort's Plea Deal Goes From "the President did nothing wrong And Paul Manafort will tell the truth" to "the president did nothing wrong".
② Right Mr. President! Glad I work For A Man who tells the TRUTH!
①, Rudy! I Know All About Flippers like Manafort! They will say Anything! They don't care About the TRUTH!

Trump Denies Heavy Death Toll in Puerto Rico From Hurricane Maria in 2017, Falsely Accusing Democrats of Inflating the Toll And A Possible Hypothetical Added Scenario to Support His Theory

Donald J. Trump
@ realDonaldTrump

Sept. 13, 2018

①... This was done by the Democrats in order to make me look as bad as possible. IF a person died For any reason, like old age, just add them on to the list Bad politics. I love Puerto Rico!

Trump's Manafort Nightmare - As His Former Campaign Chairman Paul Manafort Makes A Plea Deal With Possible Mueller Cooperation?
Sept. 14, 2018
-Anything you want to Know!
-But no white prison socks! Some grey Nagrani Italian made silk socks would help my MEMORY!

The International Space Station Captures Images of Hurricane Florence Approaching U.S. East Coast & President Trump Lashing Out At Attorney Gen. Jeff Sessions & U.S. Justice Dept. to Investigate Anonymous Op-Ed Sent to New York Times   Sept. 10, 2018

A Telegraph Operator in Titanic's Wireless Room Moments before Power Went Out Symbolizes Below Conclusion of Anonymous Op-Ed Sent by W.H. Official to New York Times!

"Should the president simply stay or be kept-out of the way, it seems the "adults in the room" will do what's right."

September 10, 2018

The Possible Rise & Fall of Trump's Lie Detector Plan To Catch The Anonymous W.H. Official Who Sent the Op-Ed to The New York Times Following Sen. Rand Paul's Remark President Trump Would be "justified" in using lie detector tests
Sept. 7, 2018
① Rand! I appreciate your fantastic loyalty during these times! What's up!
② Mr. President — the lie detector test is your dream weapon!
③ Sounds terrific! Do you think you can introduce a bill that would protect the President from having ever to take such a test in the interest of NATIONAL SECURITY!
④ Better forget it!

Trump's Impeachment Nightmare the Night He Retorted to Obama's – Our Democracy Depends On Your Vote" Speech By Saying "I've Found he's very good, Very good For *Sleeping*"
Sept. 8, 2018

Trump's Tweet In Response To The New York Times Publishing An Anonymous Op-Ed Essay That Was Highly Critical Of Him Whose Identity is Known By The Times -
Rudy Giuliani, President Trump's Attorney Responds
September 5, 2018

Donald J. Trump
@ realDonaldTrump

Does the so-called "Senior Administration Official" really exist, or is it just the Failing New York Times with another phony source? If the GUTLESS Anonymous person does indeed exist, the Times must, for National Security purposes, turn him/her over to government At once!

Trump's Possible Response To The Answer His Below Supreme Court Nominee Gave to Questions On Whether A President Can Pardon Himself or someone He Makes A Loyalty Deal With And Whether A President Can be Investigated or Subpoenaed to Testify...

September 5, 2018

FBI Director James Comey's Last Loyalty Dinner At The Trump White House
April 13, 2018
① Enjoy your salad! Sometimes life is like a salad, full of unexpected things. That's why a man needs loyal friends. Will you be my loyal friend? And if it's OK can you tell me if I am under investigation?
③ We'll see what happens. Enjoy your veal parmigiana. Beats Louie's in the Bronx!
② Mr. President you are not under investigation and I will be loyal to telling you the truth. Can I stay on as FBI Director?

Trump's Possible Thoughts As He Considers Where To Stash Away More Than 100,000 Pages of Bret Kavanaugh's Records Received From Bush (43) White House Ahead of Confirmation Hearing
September 1, 2018

How Trump Could Possibly Handle A Supreme Court Fight Against A Mueller Subpoena To Force Him to Testify In the Russia Investigation - September 3, 2018

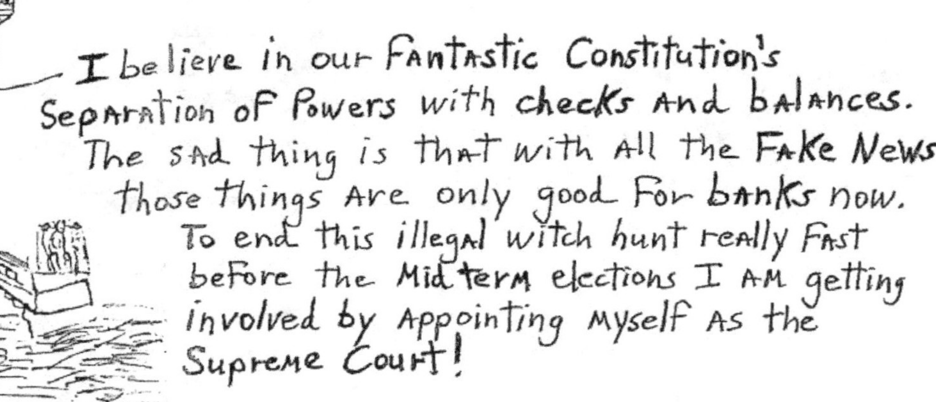

I believe in our Fantastic Constitution's Separation of Powers with checks and balances. The sad thing is that with all the Fake News those things are only good for banks now. To end this illegal witch hunt really fast before the Midterm elections I am getting involved by appointing myself as the Supreme Court!

Trump's Moscow Nightmare Possibly Caused By Justice Dept. Official Bruce Ohr's Allegation
He was told by Dossier Author that Russia "Had Trump Over A Barrel." August 29, 2018

ets With Kenyan President Uhuru Kenyatta In The Oval Office August 27, 2018
rumpets A Preliminary Trade Deal With Mexico & Recent Gains In Stock Markets Possibly
Thoughts of Business Ties To Kenya In Future
① Well, Everything I said was going to happen, it ends up happening!
② I hope you will share the wealth with Kenya!
③ We'll bring that over to Kenya...
④ In it's Capital City of Nairobi... →
TRUMP TOWER NAIROBI
TRUMP TOWER

Trump Says Social-Media Giants, Google, Twitter, Facebook Treading on "Troubled Territory"
August 28, 2018 - For Discriminating Against Conservatives - A Trump Tweet Coupled -
With What A Possible Trump Anti-Fake News Media Commission Could Look Like In Future

Donald J. Trump
@realDonaldTrump

Google search results for "Trump News" shows only the
viewing/reporting of Fake News Media. In other words,
they have it RIGGED, for me & others, so that ALMOST ALL
stories & news is BAD. Fake CNN is prominent
Republican/Conservative & Fair Media is shut out
illegal?

Trumps 2nd Nightmare About Allen Weisselberg, Chief Financial Officer Now Granted Immunity
In Cohen Probe - After Trump
Referred to John Dean as
A "RAT Type".
You dirty weasel RAT!, You dirty weasel RAT!
Aug. 27, 2018
Finances of Trump

Trump At W.H. Dinner For Evangelical Ministers Warns Of Grave Consequences If GOP Loses In Midterm Elections — An Excerpt From Trump's Remarks And What He Might Have Been Thinking August 27, 2018 Regarding His Legacy...

President Trump's Foreign Policy On Iran vs. Secretary Of State Mike Pompeo's On Meeting With Iranian President Rouhani And The Possible Trump Explanation In Future... Aug.7,2018

Trump Has Nightmare About Publisher of National Enquirer & Friend David Pecker's Safe That Is Said To Contain Damaging Information About him After Pecker Granted IMMUNITY
August 23, 2018

Sen. Lindsey Graham Paves the Way For Trump Firing Attorney General Jeff Sessions Which Would Compromise the Mueller Investigation By Allowing Trump to Nominate Someone Who Would Be More Sympathetic to Him Which Would Lead To A Purge of Justice Officials Who Have Oversight over the Russia Investigation — Putting Trump On Course to Becoming An American Strong Man Along With these historical Figures of Libya & Uganda —
August 23, 2018

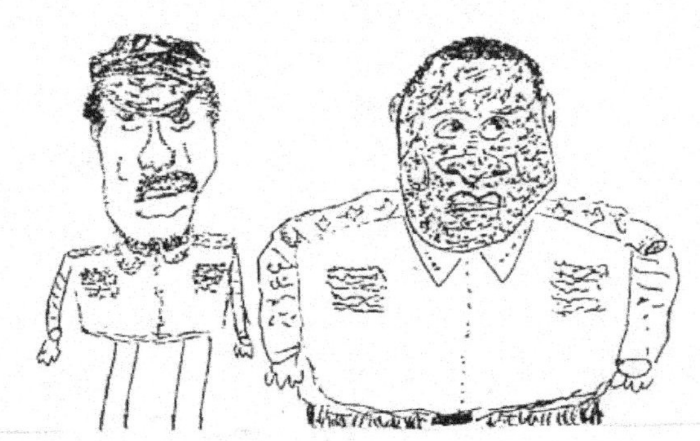

A Possible Website Ad For The Paul Manafort Legal Defense Trust Fund Launched by Friends To Assist Him With Showing the "Deep State" they cannot exert their Will on Ordinary Citizens
Aug. 23, 2018

For just one pledge of $845.00 Paul can proudly walk into his next Court House Trial with the below pair of **Louis Vuitton** Alligator & Ostrich Leather Loafer shoes - Make the call today!

All contributions will remain strictly Confidential!

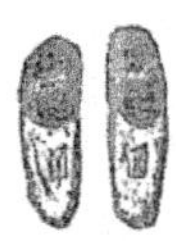

Trump Offers High Praise For His Former Campaign Chairman, Paul Manafort, Who Was Found Guilty On Eight Felony Charges   August 22, 2018

Trump's Possible Coded Message For Paul Manafort On Twitter

Trump's Possible Decoded Message For Paul Manafort

Donald J. Trump
Twitter = realDonaldTrump

I Feel very badly For Paul Manafort And his wonderful Family "Justice" took A 12 year old tax case, Among other things, Applied Tremendous pressure on him and, unlike Michael Cohen, he reFused to "break" - MAke up stories in Order to get A "deal." Such respect For A brave MAN!

I would Feel very badly For Paul Manafort iF he breaks And takes A plea deal like Michael Cohen. IF he wavers From his brave stand and decides to MAke up stories About me. I can Assure you "Justice" will put him in jail, Away From his wonderFul FAMily For A long time Anyway! In that case I certainly would not consider A pardon!

Trump Wary of "Perjury Trap," Says He Could Intervene in Mueller Probe During Interview With Reuters August 20, 2018 - And What He did <u>Not</u> Say But Might Have Been Thinking!

Trump's Lawyer Rudy Giuliani Says "Truth Isn't Truth" When Explaining Why the President Should Not Testify For Special Counsel Robert Mueller & Expounds On Perjury On Meet the Press With Chuck Todd... August 19, 2018 → How A Second Interview Might Go!

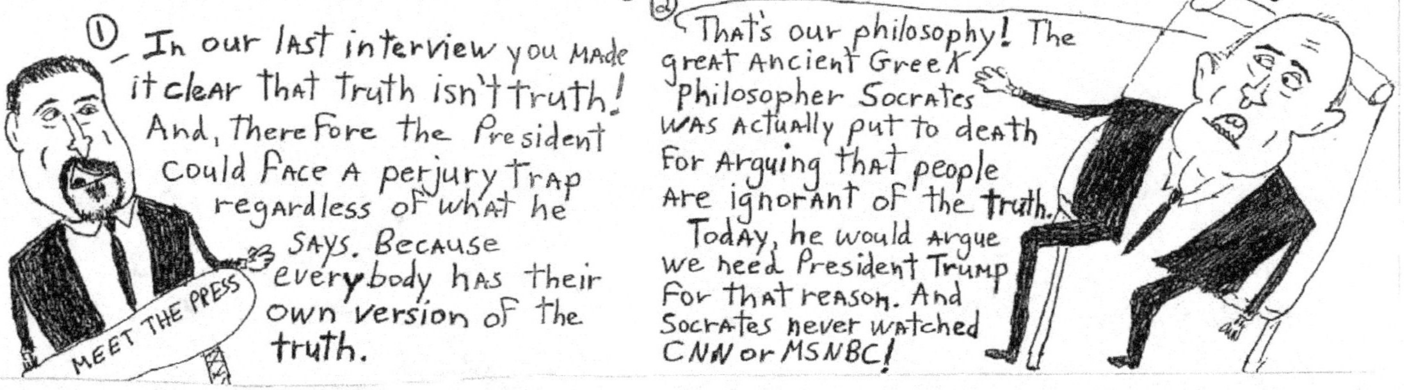

Trump Attempting To Hinder Free Speech Among Former Intelligence Leaders Who He Regards As Part Of A "Rigged Witch Hunt Deal" Speaking Out On The White House Lawn — What Old Memories Might Have Been Going On In Trump's Mind Of His Feud With Rosie O'Donnell! August 17, 2018 — As he defends Revoking Brennan's Security Clearance...

Trump Defends What Amounts to A **Huge Pinocchio** He Got From Fact Check.Org For Claiming Since he took office "the GDP [Gross Domestic Product] has **doubled & tripled**."

July 26, 2018

How A Trump-Giuliani Meeting Might Have Gone After Giuliani Threatened to "Unload" on Robert Mueller "like A ton of bricks" if the special counsel doesn't wrap up his Russia Probe by the time the Former Mayor wants him to — And Trump Pulled Former CIA Director John Brennan's security clearance...

August 15, 2018

Given Giuliani's Scortched Earth Policy On Defending President Donald Trump Like His Flip-Flopping On His Own Statements — A Possible & Conceivable Giuliani Defense Against OMAROSA MAnigault Newman's Allegation that President Donald Trump Said the N-word
August 15, 2018

FDR with FAla Aug. 8, 1940

V.P. Mike Pence's Excerpted Remarks On Trump Administration's Plan To Create A Space Force Compared To Winston Churchill's "We shall Fight on the beaches" speech on June 4, 1940 Warning Of A Possible Invasion Attempt by the Nazis

August 9, 2018

① You ask, what is our policy? I will say: It is to wage war, by Sea, land and Air, with all our Might and with all the strength that God can give us.

② Let me begin by bringing greetings from your Commander-in-chief who has been committed to strengthening American security here on Earth and in space. Speaking of space, President Trump stated clearly and forcefully that space is, in his words, "a warfighting domain, just like... land, Air, and Sea."

What Could Have Happened, Possibly In The Oval Office When Trump Watched Chris Collins (R-N.Y.) the 1st Sitting Congressman to Endorse Him Get Charged With Securities Fraud by tipping his son off About A Company's only Product That Failed A Scientific Trial   August 8, 2018

Trump's Lawyer, Rudy Giuliani Says Negotiations Between President Trump And Special Counsel Robert Mueller Seem To be Down Near the End — Giuliani's Thoughts Expressed August 8, 2018 And Not Expressed As He Stands Next To Trump Regarding the Interview

Rand Paul Visits Moscow Amid Increased Russian Sanctions Being Imposed Following the Poisoning OF An Ex-Russian Spy in the UK in March And Emerges As A Great Allie oF Trump As Moscow Applauds Paul's Efforts- August 6, 2018 After Paul Conveyed That President Trump's Hands Are now Tied By Congress Because People Are Saying -"He Loves Russia"

- We had general discussions About A lot oF issues And basically we've decided that right now we will Try to establish A dialogue And solve issues. Your biggest issue right now is there is no dialogue so we can't solve issues.

Trump's Tweet Aug. 5, 2018 Coupled With His Campaign Speech From July 27, 2016 Underscores How Motivated He Was To Get Dirt On Hillary Clinton

Donald J. Trump ✓
@realDonaldTrump

Fake News reporting, a complete fabrication, that I am concerned about the meeting my wonderful son, Donald, had in Trump Tower. This was a meeting to get information on an opponent, totally legal and done all the time in politics - And it went nowhere. I did not know about it!

July 27, 2016 - three days after the DNC email leak

Iran Says During Trump's Visit to NY in 2017 For the UN General Assembly (conFerence) Trump
Extended 8 Requests to the Iranian Team For Talks OR A Meeting with President Pouhani-
   The possible <u>not</u> reported 9th request where Trump directly Approached Pouhani in Front
OF United Nations **LAST YEAR**

Trump Speaking to the National Convention of the Veterans of Foreign Wars July 25, 2018 Against the Media for its Reaction to his Trade Tariffs Policy - With A statement on Putin He Would Have Liked to have said...

Press Secretary Sanders Defends Trump On Obstruction Of Justice For His Tweet Urging Attorney General Jeff Sessions To Stop "this Rigged Witch Hunt" Russia Probe Headed By Mueller
August 1, 2018

Trump Claims You Need **ID** To Buy Groceries In Calling For Stronger Voter ID Laws July 31, 2018
With A Possible Future Exception Story

① _We believe that only American citizens should vote in American elections, which is why the time has come for voter ID, like everything else. You know, if you go out and you want to buy groceries, you need a picture on a card, you need **ID**.
Here's a true story... which was the **only** exception. TRUE!

Trump Tweet July 31, 2018 AFter Trump Administration Settled With DeFense Distributed LAST Month That DownloAdable Blueprints For 3-D Printed Hard Plastic Guns Will Be MAde AvAilAble To The Public On August 1, 2018. These Guns Are Simple To Assemble, EAsy To Conceal And DiFFicult To Trace...

Donald J. Trump ✓
@realDonaldTrump

① I AM looking into 3-D Plastic Guns being sold to the public. AlreAdy spoke to NRA, doesn't seem to MAke Much sense!

② The Only Sense It Does MAKE —
President Donald Trump At NRA Leadership Forum MAy 4, 2018

Treasury Secretary Steven Mnuchin On The Trump Administration Granting A $100 Billion Tax Cut Mainly To The Wealthy That Would Cut Capital Gains Taxation On Investors

July 31, 2018

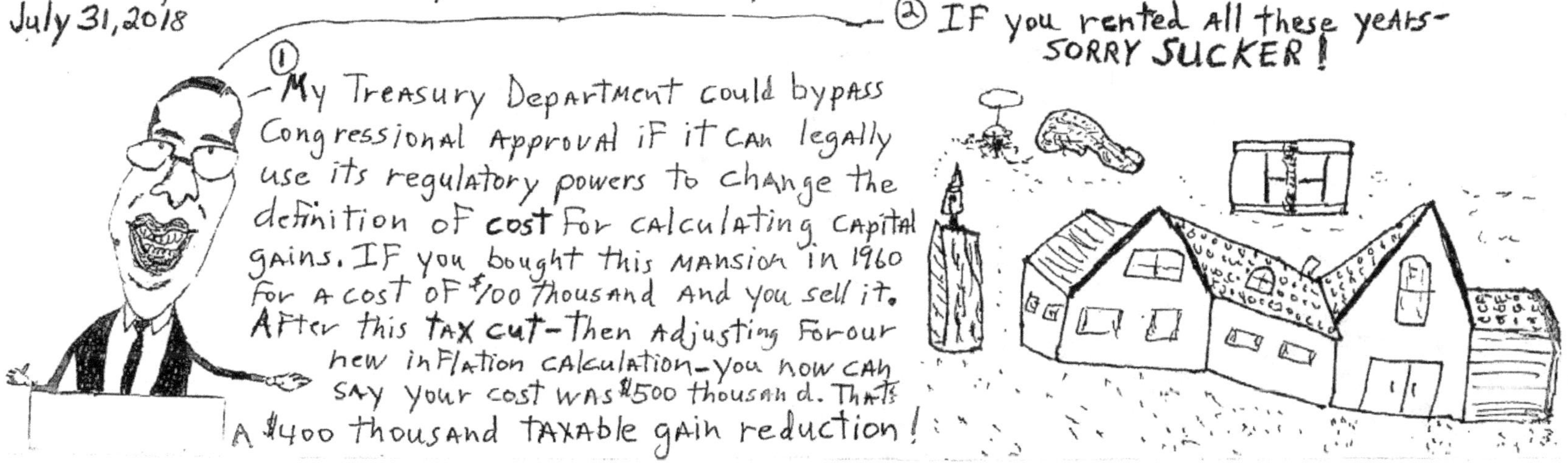

Trump Tweets He'd Shut Down Government If Democrats Don't Fund US- Mexico Wall
July 29, 2018 And What Could Come Next From His Possible Inner Thoughts

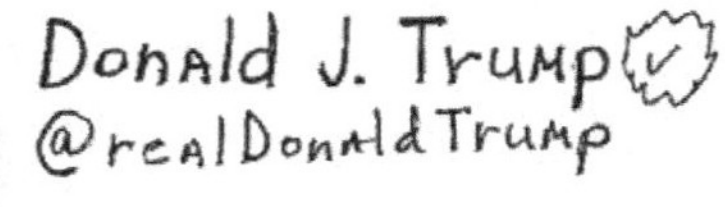

Donald J. Trump ✓
@realDonaldTrump

I would be willing to "shut" government if the
Democrats do not give us the votes for Border
Security, which includes the WALL!
     Without the votes I will shut power except
For Trump Tower — **Democrats Fault!**

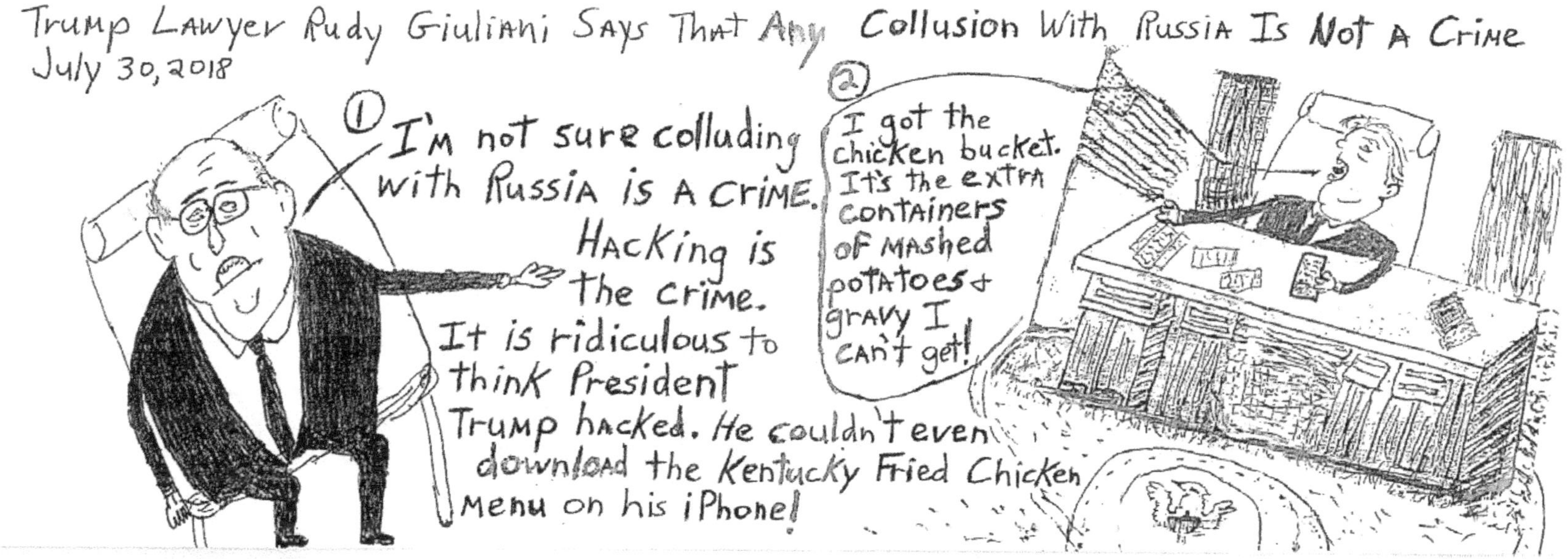

Trump Lawyer Rudy Giuliani Says That Any Collusion With Russia Is Not A Crime
July 30, 2018

Trump's Possible Reaction To Watching Supreme Court Justice Ruth Bader Ginsburg Saying She Doesn't Plan On Retiring For At Least Another Five Years   July 29, 2018

Trump Gets A Visit From The Ghost Of President Ronald Reagan Angry About His Administration's Decision To Deliver $12 Billion In Aid To Farmers Hit By Trump's Created Burgeoning Trade War July 30, 2018 - As Republicans Fume & VP Pence Stands With Trump - How It Would Have Gone -
You guys Are turning My Shining City Upon A Hill into A dArk & smelly {expletive deleted} hole!
- Mr. President we should turn this ghost over to the Putin Kremlin!

Trump & European Union Commission President Kiss In White House And Trump Tweets Picture Of Their Embrace With His Tweet July 25, 2018 that Reflects His Thoughts At The Time... ←

Donald J. Trump
@ realDonaldTrump

Trump's Inner Thoughts When Being Questioned By CNN White House Correspondent Which Resulted In Her Being Denied Access To Cover An Open Press Event At The White House   July 25, 2018
This is an Attack on our great Country by Fake News CNN!
— Mr. President, did Michael Cohen betray you?
Mr. President, Are you worried About what Michael Cohen is going to say to prosecutors?

Trump Adviser Bolton Says Putin Invitation To White House Delayed Until Mueller '**Witch Hunt**' Over After Putin Had Been Invited To White House This Fall → The Trump - Bolton Puppet Show Live From White House July 25, 2018

Secretary OF State Mike Pompeo DeFends Trump's Private Meeting With Vladimir Putin That Took Place In Helsinki Without American People Knowing About Any Results or Agreements
July 25, 2018

— The president has been clear about U.S. positions which Are the Trump Administration's positions. I had A private Meeting with Russian OFFicials And have A pretty good understanding of their private Meeting. The president And I Also had Many private Conversations. Presidents Are permitted to have private conversations with Members oF Their cabinet which Are not repeated in public. As A result oF this Meeting the President has been Assured by Vladimir Putin no Further hacking into U.S. elections by Russia will happen! **Not ever!**

Trump's Tweet July 24, 2018 Given Trump
Refused At First New Sanctions On Russia
Donald J. Trump   Until Signing off on
                                    January 30, 2018
(✓) Twitter > realDonaldTrump

I'm very concerned that Russia will be fighting
very hard to have an impact on the upcoming
Election. Based on the fact that no President
has been **tougher** on Russia than **me**, they will
be pushing very hard for the Democrats.
They definitely **don't want Trump!**

Trump On Twitter As North Korea Progresses In Building Biggest Ballistic Missile Submarine Ever- <u>Despite Promises To Trump</u>

July 23, 2018

Donald J. Trump ✓
@realDonaldTrump

A Rocket has not been launched by North Korea in 9 months. Likewise, no Nuclear Tests. Japan is happy, All of Asia is happy. But the Fake News is saying, without ever Asking Me (Always Anonymous sources), that I AM Angry because it is not going Fast enough. Wrong, very happy!

Trump Tweets Explosive Threat To Iranian President Rouhani Implying Grave & Severe Military Consequences In Response To Rouhani Who Earlier Warned Trump Not To "Play with The lion's tail" Because A War With Tehran Would Be The "Mother of All Wars" — Iranian Nuclear Scientists Possibly Giving A Thumbs Up To Trump... July 23, 2018

Trump's Press Secretary Sarah Huckabee Sanders Says President Trump Is Exploring the Mechanisms To Remove Security Clearance For Six Former Intelligence Officials — One Such Individual Is James Clapper Who Recently Confirmed Trump Was Briefed on Putin's Involvement In 2016 Election. The Mechanism Trump Might Have In Mind For Clapper — July 23, 2018

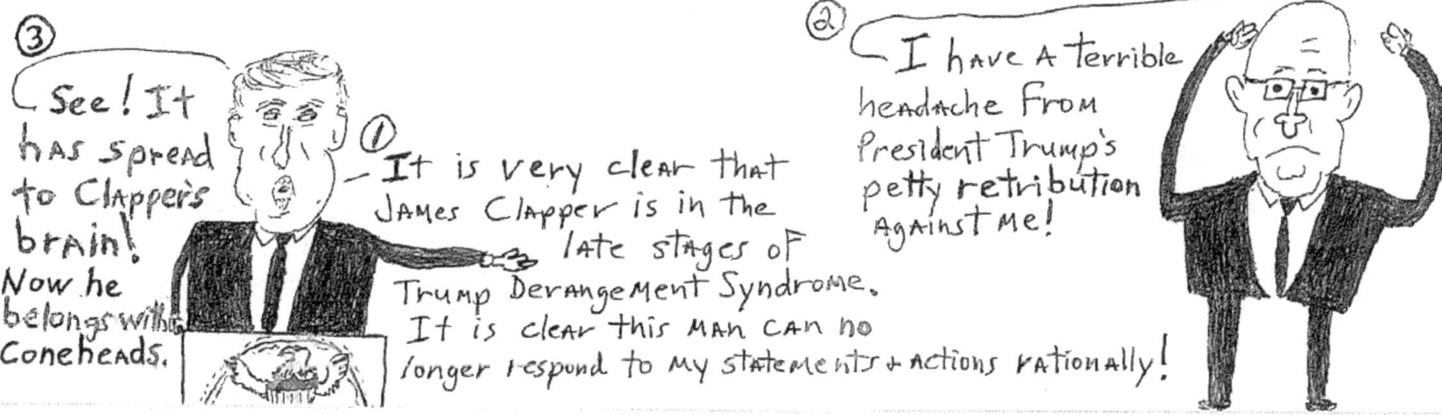

Trump Reacts To Watching His Director Of National Intelligence Dan Coats Laughing To The President's Decision To Invite Vladimir Putin To Washington In Front Of A Live Audience In Aspen Co
July 19, 2018
That {expletive deleted} Deep State Loser! We gotta find A special way to turn this Coats over to Putin this Fall!
— That's going to be special

Full speed in reverse! Let's have another shot at that iceberg!
TITANIC
Trump's Second Shot At Putin This Fall
July 19, 2018

After Three Days, Trump Rejects Putin's "Incredible Offer" To Help Russia Interrogate Americans: During The Helsinki Summit Between The Two Leaders On July 16, 2018, Putin Offered To Permit U.S Investigators To Interrogate Russians Charged With Hacking The 2016 Election, In Exchange For The United States Agreeing To Allow The Kremlin To Interrogate U.S. Citizens About Crimes Viewed As Questionable Tax Evasion Charges — WH Press Secretary Sarah Sanders July 19, 2018—

IF Trump Had It His Way

THE WHITE HOUSE

Embattled President Trump Declares His Summit With Putin A "Great Success" Except With The Real Enemy Of The People, The Fake News Media"   An Historical Comparison—

July 19, 2018

Trump Tries To Pull A U-Turn Under A Wave OF Condemnation Over His Embrace oF Putin At His Helsinki Meeting Saying He Said The Word "**Would** Instead OF **Wouldn't**" On Putin's Hacking oF the 2016 Election Plus A Server Story That Could Have Been Thought OF — July 18, 2018

Trump's Possible Thoughts As He Used A Sharpie To Cross Out The Phrase "Anyone Involved in that Meddling to Justice" Before Reading A Prepared Statement of Remarks To Walk Back His Putin Meeting Comments About Not Being Convinced That Russian Operatives Stole Democrats' emails During the 2016 Campaign — July 17, 2018 Tuesday Afternoon At the White House

Trump Commenting On His Helsinki Meeting With Putin
July 16, 2018

Trump & Putin's Joint Press Conference: Trump Answering Whether He Believes That The U.S. Is Solely Responsible As A Result Of The Mueller Probe For The Decline In U.S Relations With Russia - Trump's Inner Thoughts   July 16, 2018
(1) I hold both countries responsible. I think we've all been foolish. I think that the United States now has stepped forward, Along with Russia, And we're getting together And we have A chance to do some great things. But no collusion!
(2) Can't wait to be free of that (expletive deleted) Mueller Probe And to build my TRUMP TOWER Moscow
HELSINKI 2018
TRUMP TOWER MOSCOW
TRUMP TOWER

Trump's 2018 Version Of Gulliver's Travels By Author Jonathan Swift Published Originally
October 28, 1726 —
In 2018 Trump Travels From Washington, D.C.'s Land Of The Wimps Of
Congress To Helsinki Where He Winds Up In The Pocket
Of KGB Russian President Putin
July 16, 2018

After **Spectacularly** Caving To Putin Trump Gets A Visit From 7th U.S. President, Andrew Jackson's Ghost Then Taking His Portrait From The Oval Office & Replacing It With The Greatest Traitor To America, Benedict Arnold - Who Defected To The British During The American Revolutionary War In 1780 While A U.S. Officer...

Trump's Thoughts Before His Requested Closed & Private Meeting In Helsinki Sitting With Putin   July 16, 2018
I hope this is gonna be the Helsinki version of what happens in Vegas stays in Vegas!

White House Press Secretary Sarah Huckabee Sanders Says Chief of Staff, John Kelly Looked Sad At Trump's NATO Meeting Because He Was Expecting A Full Breakfast And There Were Only Pastries   July 11, 2018

Trump Says Meeting With Putin May Be Easier Than The NATO Summit In Brussels And His Second Stop In The United Kingdom Where He Will Meet With Prime Minister Theresa May As He Left The White House For Europe   July 10, 2018

Trump's Thoughts With His Supreme Court Nomination, Brett Kavanaugh Who Wrote In The Minnesota Law Review From 2009 – "I believe that the President should be excused from some of the burdens of ordinary citizenship while serving in office." "We should not burden a sitting President with civil suits, criminal investigations, or criminal prosecutions." "The indictment and trial of a sitting President" would "cripple the federal government."

Trump Tweets Embattled EPA Chief Scott Pruitt ⟶ Who Resigned On His Own Accord
Amid Scandals Of Legal And Ethics Nature "Has Done An Outstanding Job" July 5, 2018
Dike Failure At Tennessee Valley Authority With Ash Into Rivers
Donald J. Trump ✓
@realDonaldTrump
December 2008 ⟶
I have accepted the resignation
of Scott Pruitt as the Administrator of the
Environmental Protection Agency. Within the
Agency Scott has done an outstanding job. And
I will always be thankful to him for his efforts for
major changes in giving states & utilities more
freedom in how they dispose this TOXIC
COAL ASH from their ash ponds & state waterways here..
MAKE AMERICA GREAT AGAIN

Two Danger Moments In The History Of The World's Appeasement As Newly Obtained Evidence By U.S. Points To North Korea Is Deceiving United States On Its Nuclear Warheads Arsenal & Facilities To Make Nuclear Bombs

July 3, 2018

Donald J. Trump ✓
@ real Donald Trump

① Many good conversations with North Korea - it is going well! In the meantime, no Rocket Launches or Nuclear Testing in 8 Months. All of Asia is thrilled. IF not for Me, we would now be At War with North Korea!

②

September 30, 1938

The Legal But Outrageous Personal Connection Between Supreme Court Justice Anthony Kennedy And Real Estate Billionaire Turned President, Donald J. Trump That Overshadows Justice Kennedy's Retirement From The Supreme Court Before The Elections That Could Determine The Confirmation Of His Replacement...

July 3, 2018

Trump Begins Search For Justice Anthony Kennedy Replacement Who Announced He is Retiring On June 27, 2018 – A Possible Sign For White House Lawn

Legal Scholars Say President Donald Trump's Call For Undocumented Immigrants To Be Deported Without A Court Hearing Violates Constitutional Rights To Due Process   June 25, 2018

<u>PROTECT **OUR** COMMUNITIES</u>

Trump's Sunday June 24, 2018 Message To The European Union MAy Indicate That The U.S. Will Impose Added Tariffs On Them For Their Response To Impose Tariffs On More Than 3 Billion Worth OF U.S. goods As Retaliation For U.S. Tariffs on steel And Aluminum

Trump Signs New Executive Order To Keep Families Together Over Their Separation As Detainees At The Border
June 20, 2018 - <u>Reversing His Policy</u>

Trump Signs Executive Order To Establish the "Space Force" As Sixth Branch Of the U.S. Armed Forces Using The Term "Separate But Equal" Which Was Used In The U.S. Supreme Court's 1896 Decision To Justify Racial Segregation In "Plessy V. Ferguson, 163 U.S. 537   June 18, 2018

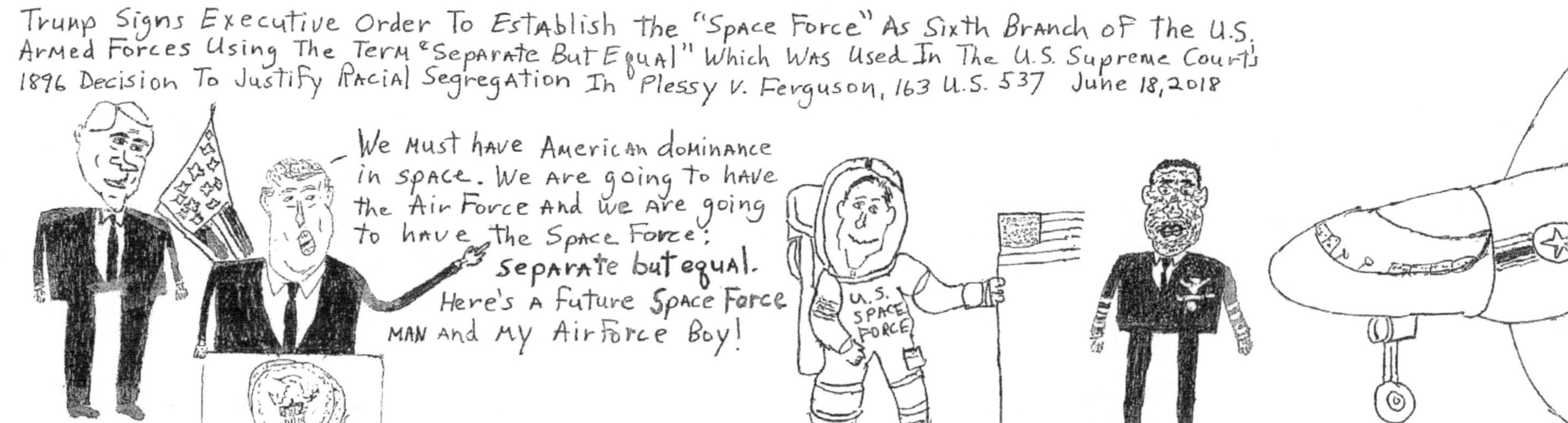

Trump Claims Parents Of Korean War Soldiers Pleaded With Him To Bring Back Remains Of Sons Killed In Korean War **65** Years Ago – On Fox News June 13, 2018

Trump Says IF He Ends Up Being Wrong About Kim Jong Un, He Probably Won't Admit It And Will Find "Some Kind OF An Excuse"   June 12, 2018 — A Possible Trump Excuse

Trump's White House Director Of Trade Policy Peter Navarro Says There Is A "Special Place In Hell" For Canadian Leader Justin Trudeay For His "We Won't Be Pushed Around" Comment After The G7 Meeting In Response To Trump Imposing Steel & Aluminum Tariffs On Canada June 10, 2018 On "Fox News Sunday".

Congress Refuses To Take Up Senator Bob Corker's Bipartisan Bill That Would Have Given Congress New Authority To Check The President's Ability To Enact Tariffs Under The Auspices of National Security

June 6, 2018

Trump Uses Inspector General (IG) Report To Spread His 'Deep State' Conspiracy Theory Based On A Revelation That FBI Agent Peter Strzok Texted To His Lover Lisa Page "We'll Stop Candidate Trump From Becoming President" And Regardless The Report Found There Was No Conspiracy Against Trump & The Report Did Not Indicate Strzok & Page Did Anything To Act On Their Text Message & Further The Report Did Not Address The Mueller Investigation As Rudy Giuliani Says On Fox News - The Investigation Has To Switch From The Trump Administration to Comey & The FBI...

June 15, 2018

Trump's Future Telephone Conversation With Putin After U.S. Sanctions Russia Over Cyber Attacks
And After Trump Calls For Its Readmission To Now The G7

Trump's School Safety Commission Won't Look At Guns, Says Education Secretary Betsy DeVos
June 5, 2018

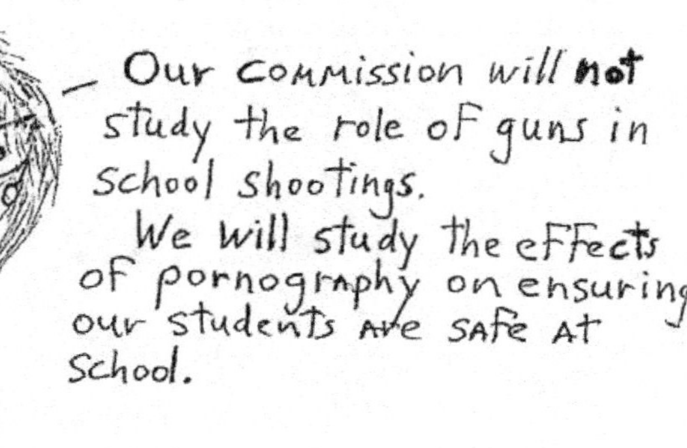

Trump Tweets That He Has the 'Absolute Right to Pardon' Himself   June 3, 2018

Donald J. Trump ✓
@realDonaldTrump

'As has been stated numerous times by these two
legal scholars & others, I have the Absolute
right to PARDON myself.

President Trump's Legal Team In A Letter In January To Robert Mueller, Special Counsel Argues That Mr. Trump Is The Country's "Chief Law Enforcement Officer" As Head Of The Executive Branch Of Our Government – Letter Released June 2, 2018 – How A Supreme Court Battle Would **Go**:

Trump's Thoughts As He Holds Up Giant Envelope, Letter From North Korea's Kim Jong Un Alongside Kim Yong Chol   June 1, 2018

President Trump Floats He Is Strongly Considering Commuting The Remaining Prison Sentence For Disgraced Former Illinois Gov. Rod Blagojevich Who Was Removed From Office On Corruption Charges Over Allegations He Solicited Bribes For Political Appointments, Including The Senate Seat Vacated By Obama When He Was Elected President In 2008 - What Blagojevich Could Be Now Thinking...
May 31, 2018

President Trump Attacks Attorney General Jeff Sessions Over Twitter After The New York Times Reported That Trump Pressured Sessions To Reverse His Decision To Recuse Himself From Oversight Of The Russia Investigation MAY 30, 2018

©2018 Richard Friedman

Trump Blames His Own Child-Separation Policy On Democrats With Respect To Taking Migrant Children From Their Parents To Deter Illegal Immigration In A Tweet Dated, May 26, 2018

© 2018 Richard Friedman

President Donald Trump Claims To Have Uncovered One Of The Biggest Spy Scandals In American History — And That The FBI, Not Russia, Is The Culprit   May 23, 2018

© 2018 Richard Friedman

Trump Casts Doubt On Historic North Korea Summit As South Korea's Moon Jae-in Travels To White House To Keep It On Track May 22, 2018

© 2018 Richard Friedman

Trump Orders Commerce Secretary Wilbur Ross To Remove Sanctions Against Chinese Phone Maker ZTE And Find Another Way To Punish It For Illegal Practices Like Violating Sanctions On Iran And North Korea MAY 13, 2018

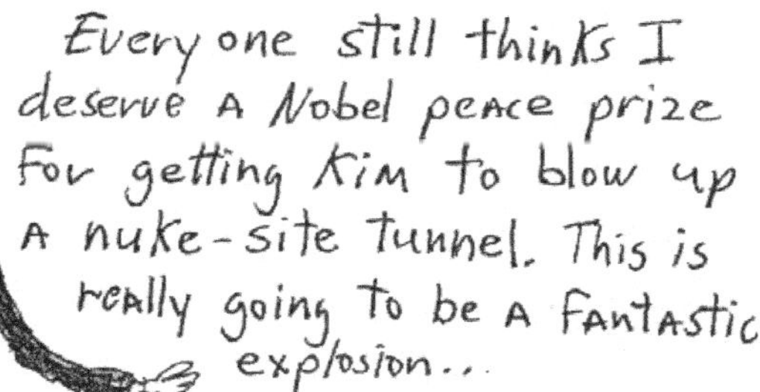

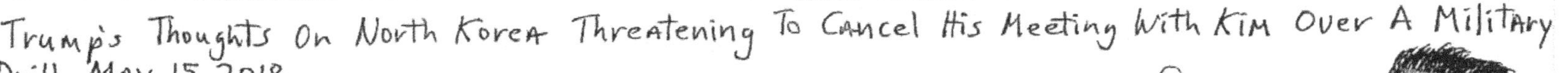

Trump's Thoughts On North Korea Threatening To Cancel His Meeting With Kim Over A Military Drill MAY 15, 2018

President Donald Trump Is Baited By North Korean Leader, Kim Jong Un Into Saying "I really think he wants to do something" And "My proudest part of this will be when we denuclearize North Korea" Upon Release of 3 Americans —
May 16, 2018 North Korea Threatens To cancel Summit
—Trump catch of day
Trump Accuses 'Obama FBI' of Spying On His Campaign Team With Informant That He Believes — Was Part of A Big "Witch Hunt" To Bring Him Down 'May 18, 2018
Nixon's Watergate
Trump's bigger than Watergate
This is bigger than Watergate
We have 3 times the crowd that Nixon got!
U.S.
U.S.

Trump Orders The Justice Department To "Look Into Whether Or Not The FBI/DOJ Infiltrated The Trump Campaign For Political Purposes MAY 20, 2018

Trump Defends His Plan To Ease U.S. Sanctions That Were Imposed On Chinese Telecommunications Giant ZTE After Company Broke U.S. Laws As Illegally Shipping To Iran Telecom Equipment That Contained U.S. Parts MAY 21, 2018

Trump Says Netanyahu's Iran Lied Speech Proves Trump Was 100% Right On Iran Deal During Joint Press Conference With Nigeria's President April 30, 2018

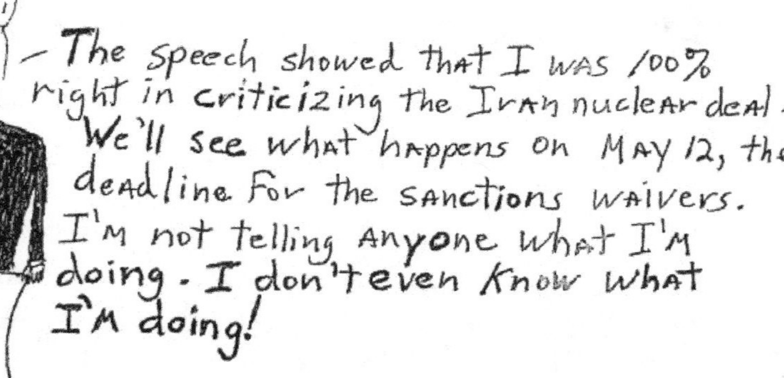

John Kelly, White House Chief Of Staff, Denies Calling Trump An 'Idiot' May 1, 2018

Trump Faces The Possibility Of A Supreme Court Battle With Mueller To Determine Whether A Special Counsel Has The Constitutional Authority To Compel A Sitting President To Testify With A Subpoena   May 1, 2018 - How It Would Go

Trump Wipes Away French President Emmanuel Macron's Shoulder Dandruff As He Welcomed Him To the White House April 24, 2018 - In Oval Office With Portrait Of George Washington

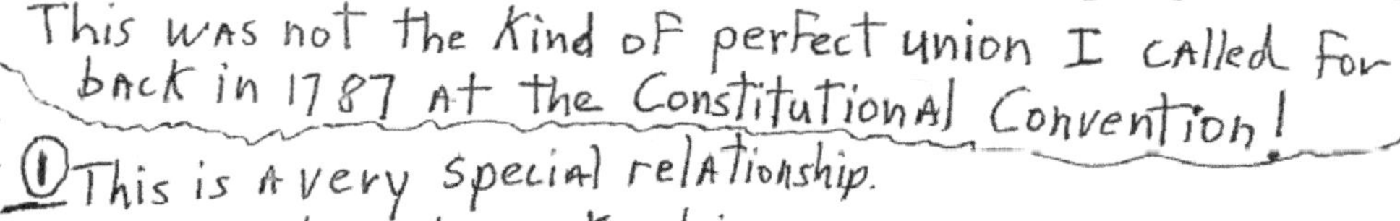

© 2018 Richard Friedman

Trump Wipes Away French President Emmanuel Macron's Shoulder Dandruff As He Welcomed Him to the White House April 24, 2018 - In Oval Office With Portrait of George Washington
This was not the Kind of perfect union I called for back in 1787 At the Constitutional Convention!
This is A very special relationship. We have to make him perfect. He is perfect!
© 2018 Richard Friedman
Trump Yells Out Threats Against Justice Department With Call-In To FOX & FRIENDS April 26, 2018
I have taken the position that I will not be involved with the Justice Department. But At some point I won't...
Mr. President! I can't stop the investigation! I need to be your new Attorney General At this point!
© 2018 Richard Friedman

Trump Talks About Firing Special Counsel Mueller After FBI Raid On His Personal Lawyer Angers the President April 10, 2018

Trump Picks His White House Doctor Navy Rear Adm. Ronny Jackson To Head Veterans Administration March 29, 2018 Jackson Holds Press Conference

Trump Says That He Does Not Expect Michael Cohen, His Long-Time Personal Lawyer To Flip After FBI Raid On Cohen's Offices   April 21, 2018

Donald J. Trump ✓ @ realDonaldTrump

Sorry. I don't see Michael Flipping despite this horrible Witch Hunt...

© 2018 Richard Friedman

Former NYC Mayor Rudy Giuliani Joins Trump's Personal Legal Team To End Mueller Probe   April 19, 2018

© 2018 Richard Friedman

— I'm doing it because I hope we can negotiate an end to this for the good of the country. This is the greatest attack on our country since 9/11. Instead of the World Trade Center it's now an attack on TRUMP TOWER!

Trump At Press Conference With Leaders Of Baltic States On Honduras Migrants Headed To The Mexican-U.S. Border   April 3, 2018

James Comey, Former FBI Director Compares Trump To A Mob Boss In His Book, A Higher Loyalty   April 12, 2018

Nikki Haley, U.S. Ambassador To The United Nations Pushes Back Against White House Claim That She Experienced "Momentary Confusion" Over the Future of Additional Russia Sanctions In Response to Russia's Failure To Rid Syria of Chemical Weapons   April 17, 2018
— I do not get confused
© 2018 Richard Friedman
Trump Floats Idea of Replacing Attorney General Jeff Sessions With Embattled EPA Head Scott Pruitt Who Says He Wants The Job — His Private Thoughts!   April 5, 2018
① Scott you Are A Fantastic person! How About replacing Sessions As Attorney General
② Sounds GREAT Mr. President
③ IF that Paul Manafort doesn't want jail time he better do A 50 dollar A - night rent deal with me on his big Trump Tower Condo
TRUMP TOWER
TRUMP TOWERR
© 2018 Richard Friedman

Trump About To Board Air Force One Is Asked IF He Still HAS Confidence In His EPA Chief Scott Pruitt April 5, 2018

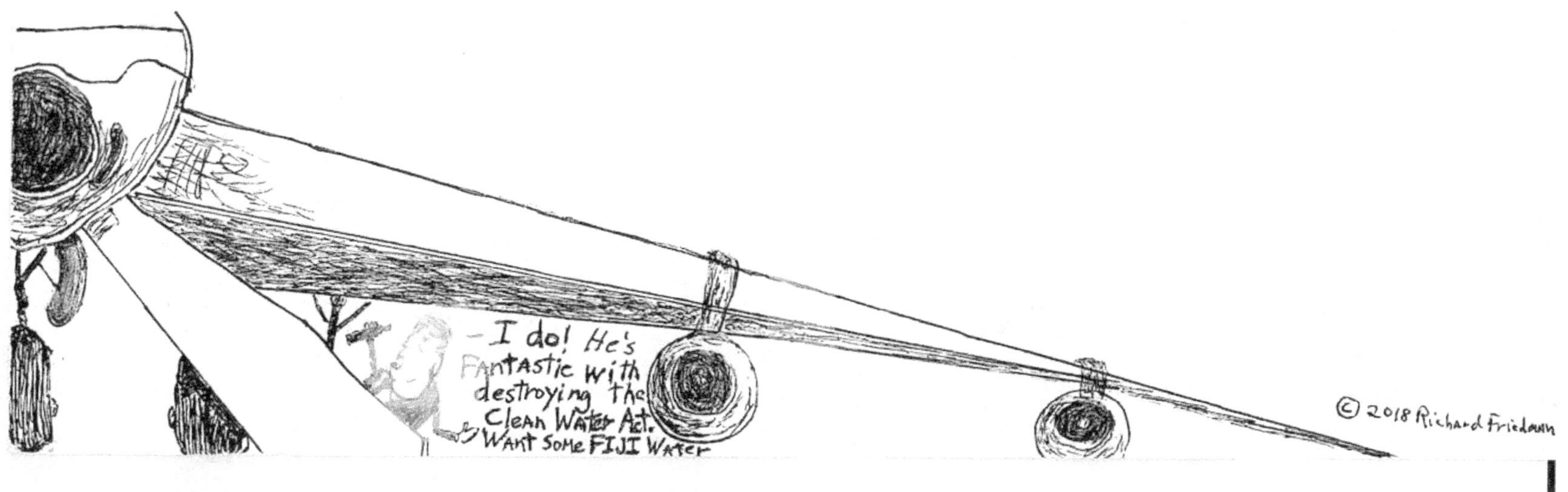

Trump Says Former FBI Deputy Director Andrew McCabe's Firing TWO Days Before He WAS To Retire With Pension Is A "Great Day For Democracy" March 18, 2018

©2018 Richard Friedman

Trump Takes Action After Pentagon Refuses To Build The Wall From Its Own Funds
March 28, 2018
© 2018 Richard Friedman
This side goes for the Wall! No More Pentagon Stuff!
Now it's the Quadagon!
March 27, 2018
© 2018 Richard Friedman
Trump Gets A Presidential Order To Sign While Watching An Important Roseanne Revival Show
②
Mr. President you just signed off on an increase of 50,000 U.S. troops in Syria
① John, I told you this new Roseanne Revival Show is top priority. Now what the {expletive deleted} did I just sign?

Trump's EPA Chief Scott Pruitt Under Investigation For Non-Government Trips And Huge Expenses For EPA-Funded Security - Below His Family Vacation At Disneyland
② Stay Away! Security check out a suspicious mouse in front of the Disney Castle!
① Dad there's Mickey Mouse!
③ What's your name Mouse?
④ Mickey
Ⓔ 2018 Richard Friedman

Trump Says U.S. Will Withdraw From Syria Very Soon In Ohio Speech March 29, 2018
Ⓒ 2018 Richard Friedman
BUILDING A STRONGER AMERICA
- We're Knocking the hell out of ISIS. Let the other people take care of it now. Like these good folks...

Trump Furious Over Leak of Sensitive Notes Warning Him Not To Congratulate Putin
March 21, 2018
-Who!
There's going to be A SCALP over this!
I don't know yet. But I AM going to start practicing on this Mexican!
© 2018 Richard Friedman

Trump Tells Reporters On Air Force One His Embattled EPA Chief Scott Pruitt Has Done A Fantastic Job
April 5, 2018   © 2018 Richard Friedman
-I think he's done Ah incredible job. He's been very courageous. It hasn't been easy wiping out All those Obama regulations that protected people Against All those dangerous poisons in our environment! For rolling back rules requiring cars to be cleaner he deserves his new Cadillac Escalade From GM

Trump Says He'll Leave Kim Jong Un Meeting If It Isn't Fruitful And Rehearses Plan With New National Security Advisor John Bolton   April 19, 2018

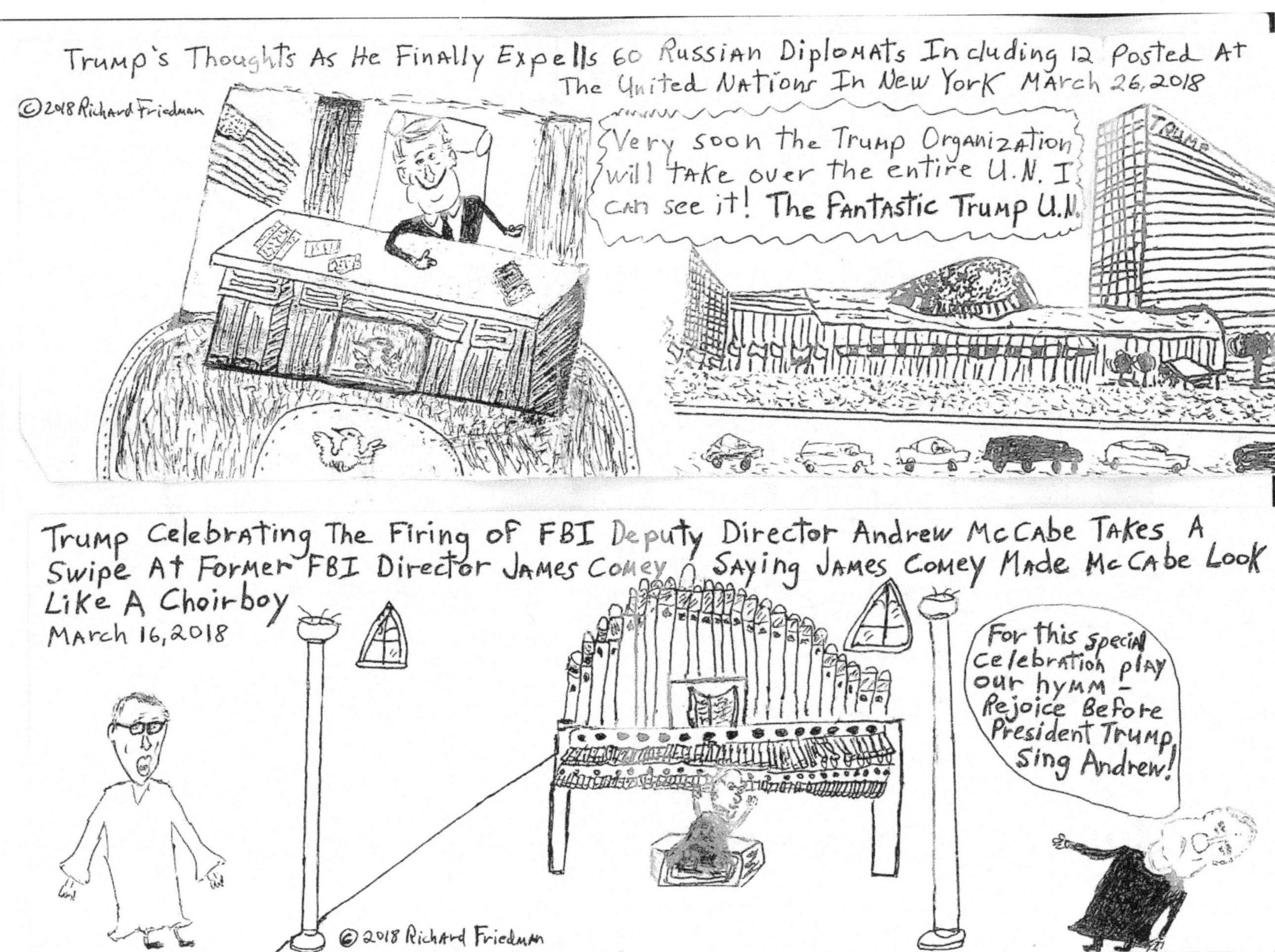

Trump's Thoughts As He Finally Expells 60 Russian Diplomats Including 12 Posted At The United Nations In New York March 26, 2018
©2018 Richard Friedman
Very soon the Trump Organization will take over the entire U.N. I can see it! The Fantastic Trump U.N.
TRUMP
Trump Celebrating The Firing of FBI Deputy Director Andrew McCabe Takes A Swipe At Former FBI Director James Comey Saying James Comey Made McCabe Look Like A Choirboy
March 16, 2018
For this special celebration play our hymm - Rejoice Before President Trump Sing Andrew!
©2018 Richard Friedman

Rachel Brand Resigns From No.3 Position At Justice Dept. The Same Night Trump Refuses To Release Democratic Memo That Was In Response to Nunez Memo Which Had Been Designed To Pave The Way For No.2 Position At Justice Rod Rosenstein To Be Fired By Trump Friday Night Feb. 9, 2018

Trump's U.S. Treasury Secretary Mnuchin Says Russia Sanctions Are Coming After The Telephone Book Like Release of Russian Billionaires And Top Russian Officials Close To Putin January 30, 2018 — As Trump Administration Fails To Enforce Sanctions Passed By Congress Against Russia...

President Donald Trump Releases WH Photo To Show The Nation
That He Was Hard At Work At His Desk This Past Weekend
After The Government Shut Down Jan. 20, 2018 — Here he is
Calling in An order To WH Staff For Fried Chicken

Trump Says 'Unlikely' He Will Need To Testify In Mueller Probe oF Russian InterFerence In
U.S. Election Jan. 10, 2018 — Repeatedly Using "No Collusion"...

Trump Compares His Attorney General Jeff Sessions To Mr. Magoo, A Bumbling Cartoon Character As Prosecutor Mueller Investigates — Feb. 2018

Trump Balks At Immigration Deal That Would Include Protections For Haitians & Africans Jan. 11, 2018

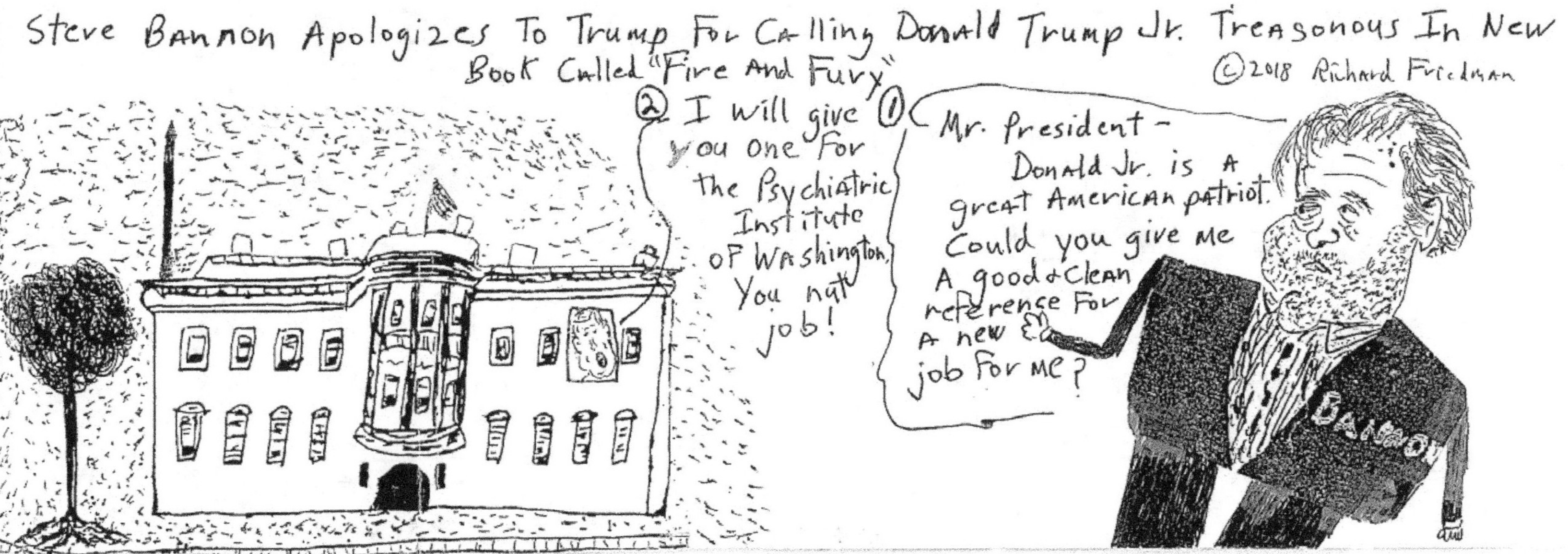

Steve Bannon Apologizes To Trump For Calling Donald Trump Jr. Treasonous In New Book Called "Fire And Fury"
© 2018 Richard Friedman
② I will give you one for the Psychiatric Institute Of Washington, You nut job!
① Mr. President – Donald Jr. is a great American patriot. Could you give me a good & clean reference for a new job for me?
BANNON

Jared Kushner Loses Top-Secret Security Clearance To High Level Intelligence Information And Expands On His Real Job At The White House   March 2, 2018 © 2018 Richard Friedman
KUSHNER REAL ESTATE GROUP
Headquarters 666 Fifth Avenue
New York City, New York
2nd Floor East Wing
INVESTORS WELCOMED

Trump At Meeting With Governors On Gun Control After Parkland School Shooting Say Not To Be Afraid Of NRA "They Are On Our Side" Feb. 26, 2018
Over the weekend I met with NRA CEO Wayne La Pierre. I told him we gotta do something It went FANTASTIC!
① We gotta do something
③ Let's open Mental Institute For 18 to 20 year old
② OK but 18 year olds must be able to buy Automatic Assault weapon
© 2018 Richard Friedman
House Speaker Paul Ryan's Circus Tight Rope Act Telling Reporters He Wants Public Release Of Nunez Memo Which Alleges FBI Abused Its Surveillance Tools Against Trump - His Circus Act Jan. 30, 2018
NUNEZ MEMO
FAKE NEWS
REAL NEWS
We need to Keep this Memo separate From the Mueller Trump Investigation
© 2018 Richard Friedman

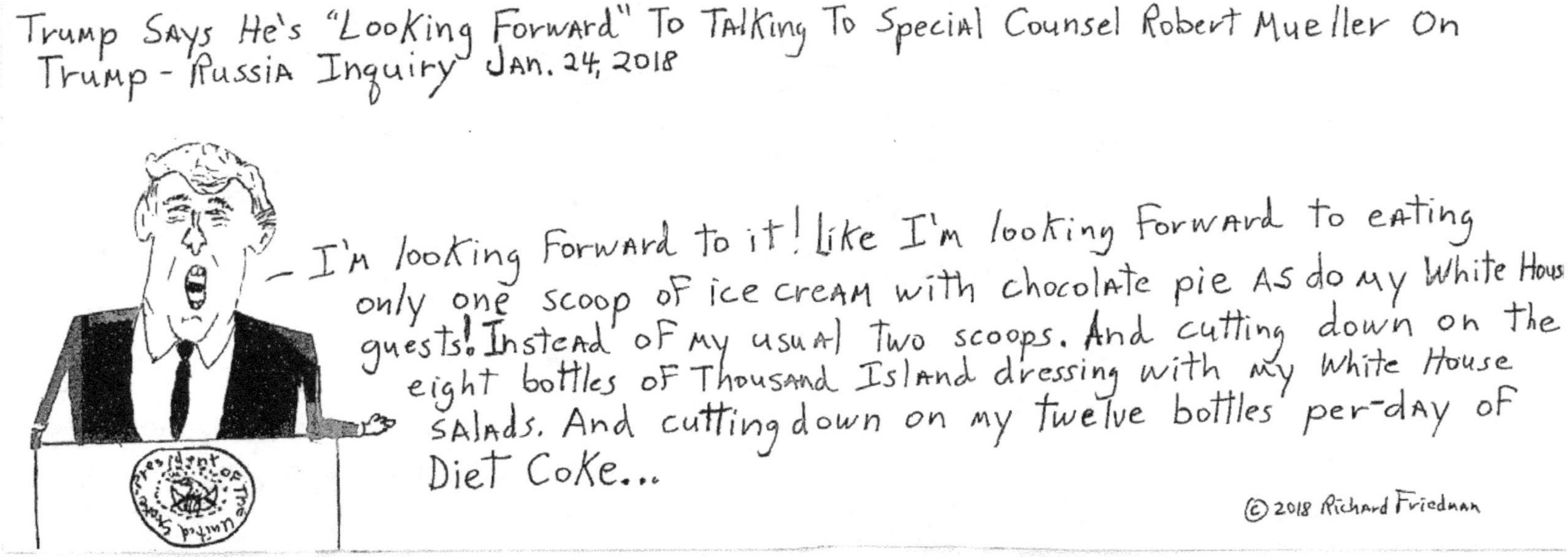

Trump Says He's "Looking Forward" To Talking To Special Counsel Robert Mueller On Trump - Russia Inquiry Jan. 24, 2018

© 2018 Richard Friedman

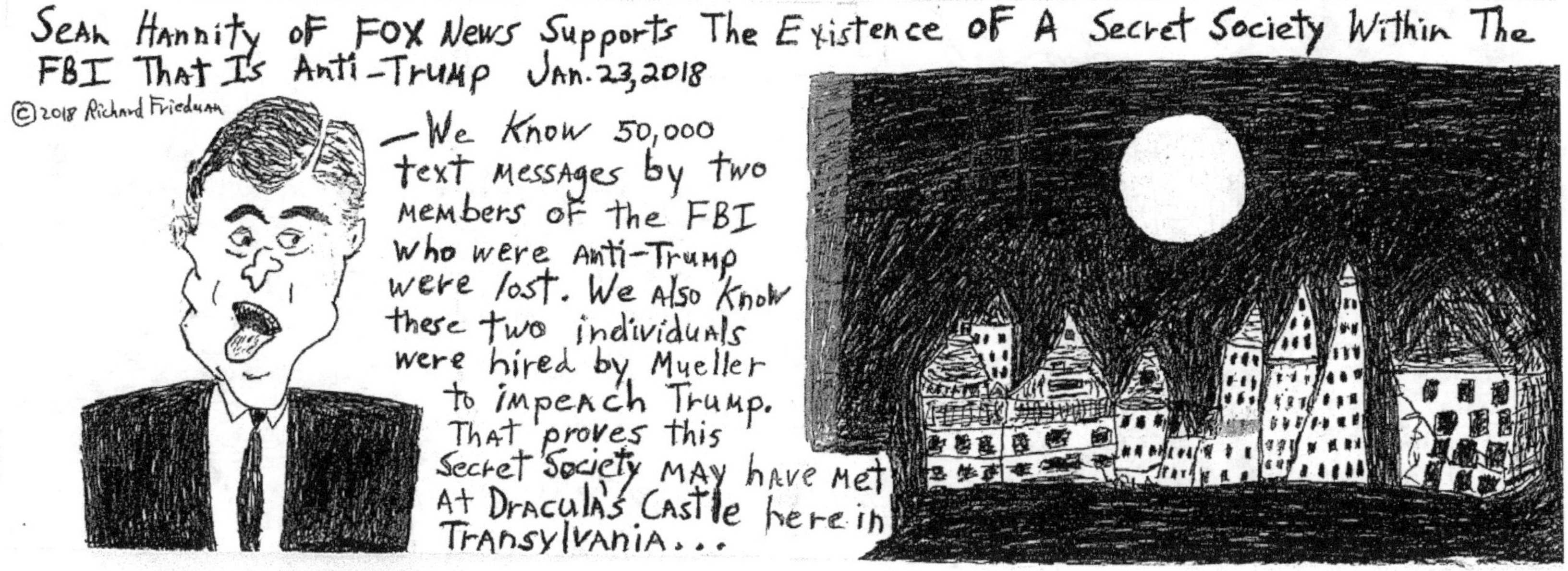

Sean Hannity of FOX News Supports The Existence Of A Secret Society Within The FBI That Is Anti-Trump Jan. 23, 2018

© 2018 Richard Friedman

Trump Says Take Guns First From Crazy People And Due Process Of Law Can Come Later
Feb. 28, 2018
— With Former Vice-President Cheney here it would be too dangerous to take his gun First. I would just imprison him. He never spoke up For me Anyway... Very Sad. Maybe Guantanamo!
© 2018 Richard Friedman
Secretary of State Rex Tillerson's Inner Thoughts After Being Fired On Twitter BeFore Being Told By Trump Just BeFore Giving His Statement At The State Department 3/13/2018
Sure glad I have my pension From Exxon-Mobil! Glad I'm not Former deputy FBI director Andrew McCabe who may get Fired 2 days before he can collect his. And wind up like this...
FIRED TRUMP CABINET MEMBER NEED FOOD
© 2018 Richard Friedman

Trump Says Reports of Chaos In The White House Is FAKE NEWS   March 6, 2018

Trump Says Top Law Firms Want To Represent Him In Russia Case Inquiry   March 25, 2018
© 2018 Richard Friedman

Trump Defends Congratulatory Call To Putin On Winning Reelection MARCH 21, 2018

Trump Goes To WAR As John Bolton Becomes National Security Adviser   March 22, 2018

Trump Budget Director Mick Mulvaney Says John Kelly Is Definitely Not Getting Fired Over Kelly's Handling Of The Resignation Of WH Staffers Accused Of Abuse By Their Ex-Wives Feb.11,201

— I think all the stories about replacing Gen. Kelly are from these people who are unhappy they've lost access to the president...

© 2018 Richard Friedman

Trump's Sec. of Commerce Wilbur Ross Defends Trump's Plan To Raise Tariffs On Imported Steel & Aluminum And Possibly Start A Trade War With Other Countries March 6, 2018

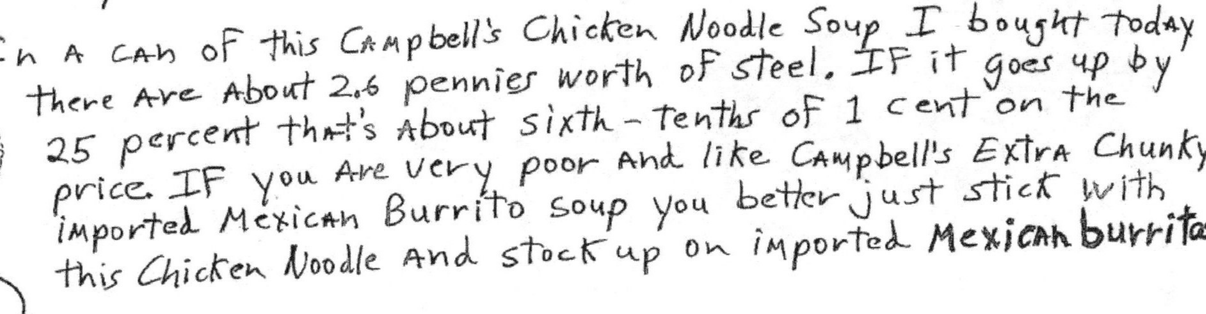

— In a can of this Campbell's Chicken Noodle Soup I bought today there are about 2.6 pennies worth of steel. If it goes up by 25 percent that's about sixth-tenths of 1 cent on the price. If you are very poor and like Campbell's Extra Chunky imported Mexican Burrito soup you better just stick with this Chicken Noodle and stock up on imported Mexican burrito

© 2018 Richard Friedman

Trump Warns of 'Phase Two' Against North Korea
If Sanctions Don't Work   Feb. 23, 2018
Phase Two of the
U.S. Strategy Against
North Korea will be
Very, very unfortunate
For the world here...
© 2018 Richard Friedman
PHASE 2

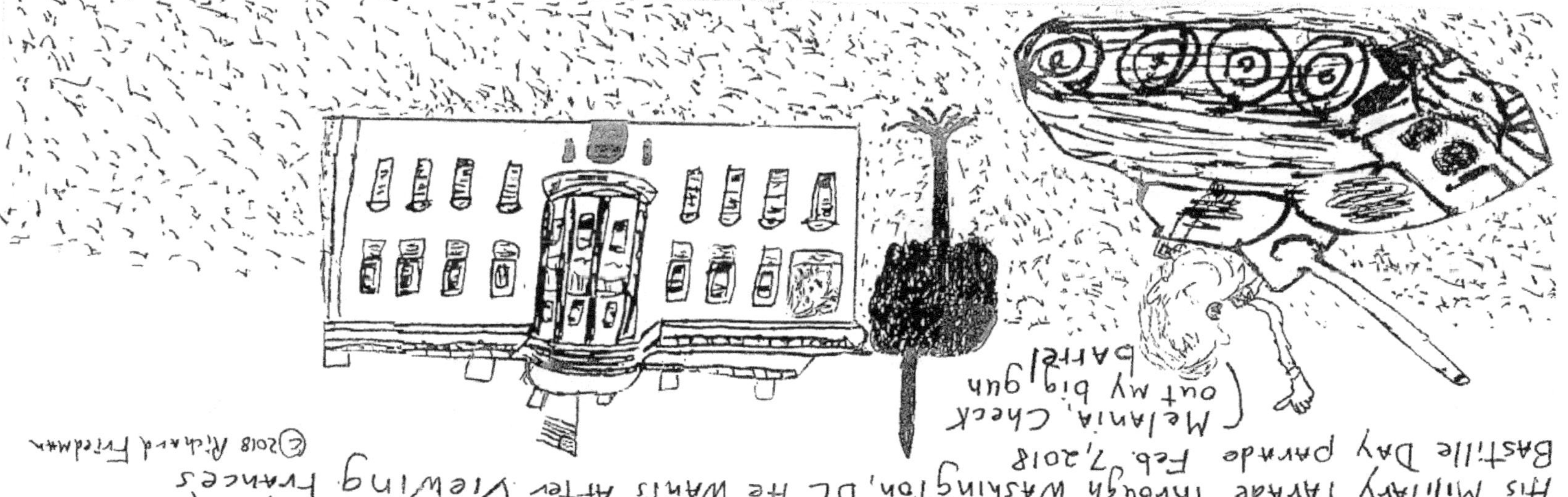

Melania, Check
out my big gun
barrel
Trump Picks Out His Tank And Parades Around White House In Preparation For
His Military Parade Through Washington, DC He Wants After Viewing France's
Bastille Day Parade   Feb. 7, 2018
© 2018 Richard Friedman

President Trump Upon Receiving Word From South Korean Official That North Korea's Leader, Kim Jong Un Has Extended An Invitation For A Meeting With Trump Has A Vision March 8, 2018

Intelligence Report On How Israel Discussed Exploiting Trump Son-In-Law Jared Kushner Feb. 27, 2018

Trump Says If White House Chief of Staff & Former Marine Corps. General John Kelly Was A Teacher Armed With A Gun He Could Have Stopped A School Shooter   Feb. 22, 2018

© 2018 Richard Friedman

Trump's Plan To Replace Food Stamps With Food Box Delivery Program   Feb. 12, 2018

© 2018 Richard Friedman

Trump Denies Wanting To Arm Teachers Feb. 22, 2018 After White House Meeting
With Survivors & Parents of School Shooting

#1 #2 #3 #4 #5

- What I said was give concealed guns to gun adept teachers with military or special training experience. Only the best which would amount to 20% or 1 out of 5 say of these here teachers... In this case it's clear who would deter the savage sicko! Art Teacher #4 has the Ability!

KILL

©2018 Richard Friedman

Trump On China's President Xi Jinping Becoming President For Life At Fundraiser In Florida And China Banning Winnie the Pooh For Looking Like President Xi Jinping March 1, 2018
©2018 Richard Friedman

- He's now president for life, president for life. And he's great. And look, he was able to do that. I think it's great. Maybe we'll have to give that a shot someday. IF President helps with North Korea we could also take a shot at Winnie the Pooh...

Trump Praises Rep. Devon Nunez For Writing The Memo The President Says
Vindicates Him And Throws In An Endorsement From The
Ghost Of John Wayne Feb. 3, 2018
© 2018 Richard Friedman

Trump Calls Putin To Congratulate Russian President On His Election Win   March 20, 2018
© 2018 Richard Friedman

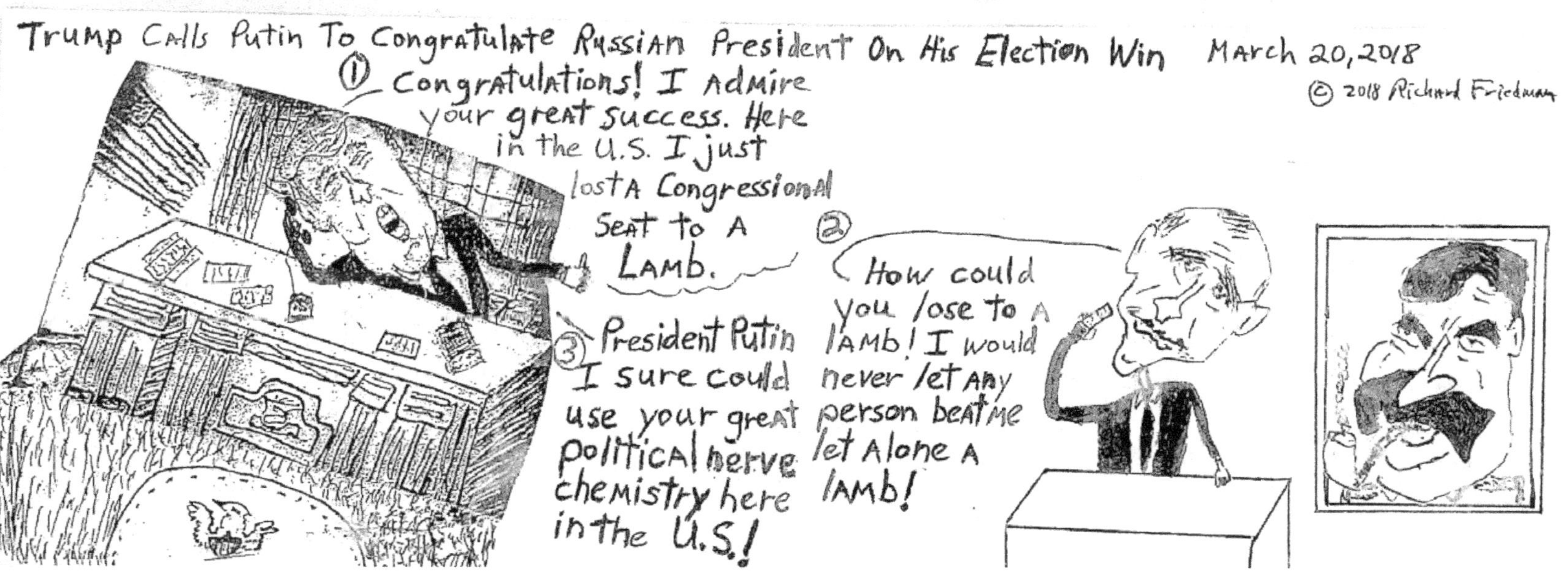

Jared Kushner & Trump In The W H Situation Room A Month After Qataris Said No To A 500 Million Dollar Loan To Kushner's Family On Its Financially Distressed 666 5th Ave Propert

① Mr. President, with all its tons of oil money Qatar would not loan my family a (expletive deleted) dime. And you recently did your anti-terrorism gig in Saudia Arabia. Qatar's only land border is with Saudia Arabia. Check out my map here! IF the Saudis close their border we can starve the (expletive deleted) And if we could get Saudia Arabia to denounce Qatar as a supporter of terrorist groups. You got it made! We might even start a Mid-East War!

© 2018 Richard Friedman

② Sounds Fantastic Jared! Sure glad I put you in charge of Mid-East peace!

Trump At Press Conference With Swedish Leader Minimizes Russian Interference In U.S. Elections At White House March 6, 2018

The Russians had no impact on our votes, but certainly there was meddling and probably there was meddling from other countries and individuals. It could have been this dude in the Congo with his new two transistor radio...

© 2018 Richard Friedman

2. The First Year (2017)

The Trump Administration Frustrated By Leaks Orders Sean Spicer To Collect All Electronic Devices From Communication Staffers
February 26, 2017

President Trump On Truth Serum Sodium Thiopental — What He Would Have Said About Secretary Of State Rex Tillerson For Calling Him A Moron On July 19, 2017

Trump Tosses Paper Towels Into A Crowd Of Puerto Rican Hurricane Victims In Guaynabo Puerto Rico Oct. 3, 2017

WH Press Sec. Sarah Huckabee Defends WH Chief of Staff John Kelly's Defense of Trump Claim That Rep. Frederica Wilson Took Credit In 2015 For Funding An FBI Building 10/20/2017

Kelly Anne Conway Defends Donald Trump Jr's Meeting With A Kremlin Attorney To Get Information Damaging To Hillary Clinton During Campaign July 10, 2017

Top Trump Aide KellyAnne Conway About New CIA Proof Putin Gave Orders That Russian Hackers Infiltrate U.S. Election In Favor Of Trump June 22, 2017

Ex-Trump Campaign Adviser Says Papadopoulos Was Just A 'Coffee Boy' After Papadopoulos Pleaded **Guilty** To Making **False** Statements To The FBI About Interactions With Foreign Officials **Close** To The Russian Government Oct. 31, 2017

Here's a photo given to me from the White House showing Papadopoulos working as a coffeeboy for a dinner between Trump and then-Alabama Sen. Jeff Sessions during a campaign meeting. He never even worked in Trump Tower.

Trump Meets With Former Secretary of State Henry Kissinger At White House Oct. 10, 2017 And Takes A News Interview

① Obama Care is Failing. Henry Kissinger here doesn't want a 116 percent cost increase in his health care & insurance.

② To be able to take a good piss I would pay 116 Million Mr. President

③ My people At Trump University Hospital could get you pissing like Niagara Falls for only 115 Million, Henry.

Treasury Secretary Steve Mnuchin Says Proposed Biggest Tax Break In History Would Greatly Benefit The Wealthy April 26, 2017 And Economic Growth Will Pay For The Plan

2017 TAX REFORM

My best Friend Sam Edelman here who worked with me at Goldman Sachs has already purchased this new yacht. Here is MY TAX BREAK 2017...

MY TAX BREAK 2017

After Obama Gets Profiles In Courage Award Trump Gets Charlton Heston Award From NRA
May 7, 2017

Trump Says His Passed Tax Cut Bill Behind Corporate Bonuses - Bill That Slashes The Corporate Tax Rate to 21 Percent From 35 Percent December 22, 2017

Trump In West Virginia Speaks To His Base Aug.3,2017 Against The Investigation Into Ties To Russia Of Him And His Administration

Trump Says He Likes Steve Bannon After Charlottesville Violence And Amid Uproar Over Trump Support Of White Supremacist Groups Protesting The Take-Down Of A Statue Of Robert E. Lee August 15, 2017

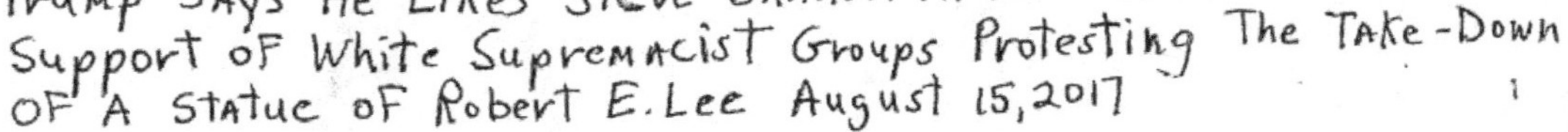

Vice President Pence On Trumps Continued Attacks On Attorney General Sessions For Recusing Himself In The Russian Investigation July 27, 2017

White House Press Sec. Sean Spicer Says Trump's 2016 Tax Returns Are Under Audit And Therefore Will Not Be Released
April 17, 2017

Former Acting Attorney General Sally Yates Testifies That the American People Had Been Misled About The Underlying Conduct OF Pres. Trump's National Security Adviser Mike Flynn May 8, 2017

I can only tell you his underlying conduct was problematic and both General Flynn and Russian President Putin enjoy horse riding.

Health & Human Services Secretary Tom Price On House Republican Healthcare Bill May 7, 2017

The president is Fulfilling his promise to the American people by giving them access and choice to the health care that they want. Take this elderly man with arthritis, prostate cancer and who has had 3 strokes why should he have to pay for birth control. If he chooses not to pay the pricing on his health care risk he can sure save a great deal of money...

White House Press Secretary Sean Spicer Defends Trump On Russian Connections   March 28, 2017

Trump Speaks From Oval Office After Republicans Pull Health Care Bill Flanked By V.P. Pence & Health Sec. Price March 24, 2017

Sen. Lindsey Graham On Trump Ordering Strike On Syrian Airfield In Response To Chemical Weapons Attack April 6, 2017

March 23, 1983

Trump Keeps It Friendly On North Korea With China President Xi At G20 In Germany July 8, 2017

White House Press Sec. Sean Spicer AFter Trump Said "We Are now Sending An ArMAdA. Very powerFul" To The Korean PeninsulA When It Was Then Heading In The Exact Opposite Direction — Towards Australia   April 19, 2017

The president said that we have An ArMAdA going towards the peninsula It is happening. We put out A release on its Final destination. We did not say when because nobody Asked us if now MeAnt now At that Moment. ThereFore the MediA jumped to the conclusion without proper questioning on the Meaning now in that context.

Vict White House Press Corps From The West Wing oF WH JanuAry 16, 2017 Back For Last Question

Trump On His Meeting With Intelligence Leaders Over Russian Hacking Of Democratic National Committee That Putin Helped Him Win The Election January 6, 2017

Trump With Puerto Rico Governor Ricardo Rossello While Visiting Following Hurricane — Praising Him Oct. 4, 2017

Trump Meets Putin At G 20 Conference In Germany- How It Went On Russian Interference In U.S. Election July 7, 2017

2 Like I just joked these Fake news people Are Against you And we must stand together in this struggle.
I will Agree to A Future dialogue on cyber security And look Forward to your next victory in 2020.

1 Mr. President the American people believe you interfered in the election And Are very concerned. Could you just state A crack down on Russian hackers in cyber-space will happen!

3 You Are right About that!

te And Sen. Mitch McConnell Are Now Very Defending Steve Bannon Who Has Declared Republican Establishment Targeting Senator :ll As Public Enemy Number One

1 Steve Bannon is A Friend of Mine. I MAy try to tAlk him out of recruiting certain GOP Primary 2018 Challengers

UNITED STATES OF AMERICA

2 What About ME you {expletive deleted}!

WANTED DEAD or ALIVE

BANNON

Trump Says That Mueller Who Is Investigating Whether Trump Obstructed Justice In Russian Probe May Have To Be Fired June 24, 2017

Mueller's long, long time Friendship with Former FBI Head Comey is very, very bothersome. Here is A portrait of them when they were in Den 201 As Cub Scouts...

Trump Says His Wealthy Friends Are Not So Happy With Him Pushing His Tax Plan In Missouri Nov. 29, 2017

These wealthy friends of mine who Are very wealthy Are not so happy with me. But that's OK... They Are happy with their new Rolls...

President Donald Trump's Fine Tuned Machine Press Conference From White House Feb. 16, 2011

Trump Prosecutor Mueller Shows Flynn His Prepared Jail Cell With Portrait of Obama Who Fired Flynn And Told Trump Not To Appoint Him   Dec. 1, 2017

Senior WH Adviser Stephen Miller Supports President Trump's Claim He Lost New Hampshire Because of Illegal Voters Being Bused From Massachusetts Feb. 15, 2017

Trump During Israeli Visit Speaks Out About Being Accused Of Giving Information From Israel To Russians About Terrorist groups loading bombs into laptops to blow up Airliners May 22, 2017

President Trump's Conversation With Sec. Rex Tillerson During Their Sword Dance During Saudi Trip MAY 20, 2007 As Fired FBI Director James Comey Says He Will Testify In Russian Probe

Trump's Lawyer Says He Wrote the President's Tweet About Flynn's Dismissal For Lying To V.P. Pence & the FBI Dec. 2, 2017

Steve Mnuchin, Trump's Treasury Man Fails To Deliver A Promised Analysis That Would Reduce The Defecit by $1 Trillion Rather Than Increase It
Nov. 30, 2017

Trump Says Texas Church Shooting Caused By Mental Health Problem Not Guns November 6, 2017 From Tokyo, Japan

Trump Rises Up To Present Pope Francis With A Set of Writings From Martin Luther King Jr. At The Vatican May 24, 2017 Along With A Bronze Sculpture of Lotus Flowers

Trump Says He Informed China's President Xi Jinping About Air Strikes Over Syria While They Were Having Their Dessert of Chocolate Cake At Mar-A-Lago In Palm Beach April 12, 2017

Homeland Security Secretary John Kelly Defends Trump's Son-in-Law Jared Kushner Following Reports He Had Attempted To Set Up A Backchannel of Communications With Russia
May 28, 2017

① — I think Any time you can open lines of communications with Anyone, whether they're good Friends or not-so-good Friends, is A smart thing to do because out of not-so-good Friends we can make good Friends...

② Let's set up A secret line of communication so we can become good Friends. I'll call you every week.

③ Let's have some Russian Borscht soup

④ Then I'll give the Kremlin the good news- This is better than Borscht

James Clapper Former Dir. of National Intelligence When Asked About If He Knew About Communications Between Russians & White House Senior Advisers Now Under Trump When He Was Director Under President Obama
May 29, 2017

— My dashboard warning lights was clearly On

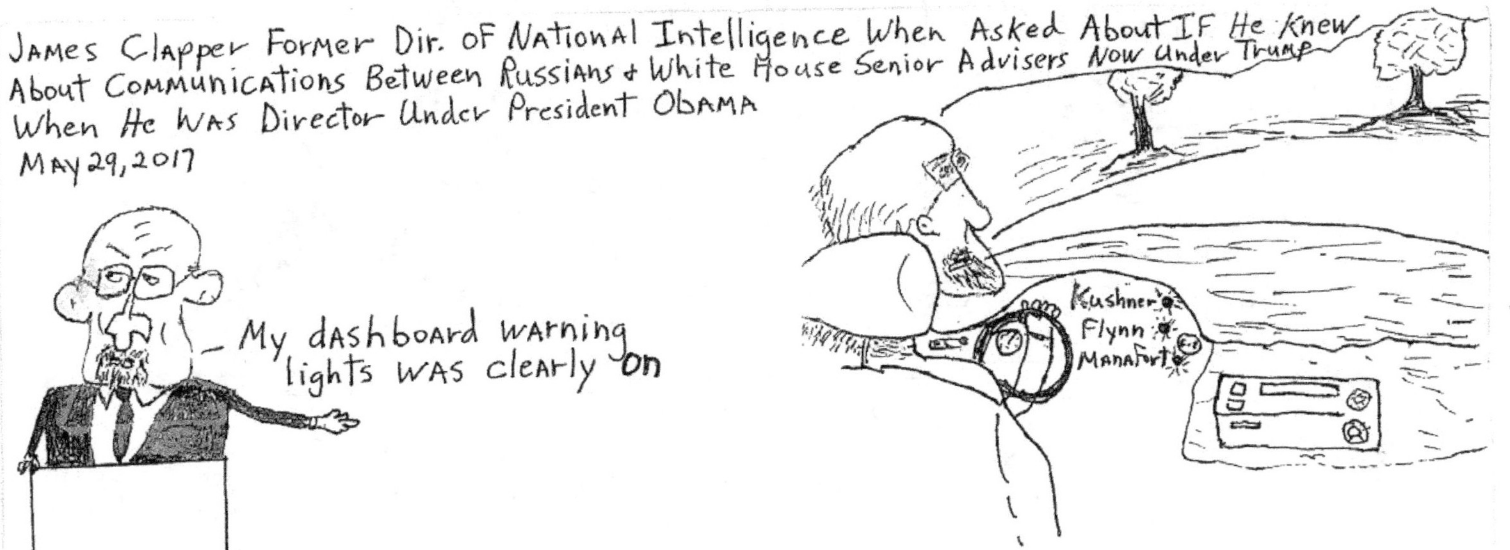

President - Elect Trump Rejects Findings OF U.S. Intelligence Agencies That Russia Engaged In Political Hacking   December 12, 2016

Trump's Economic Facts & Where He Got Them From For Withdrawing From The Paris Climate Agreement   June 1, 2017

President-Elect Trump Nominates Rick Perry To Lead The Dept. Of Energy, An Agency The Former Texas Governor Wanted To Abolish December 14, 2016

Steve Bannon, Trump's Chief Strategist Gets Fired And Is Escorted Out By McMaster And Kelly August 18, 2017

Trump Praises Crowd Size While Touring Hurricane Harvey Devastation In Texas Aug. 29, 2017
USA
What a Crowd, what a turnout! We even got these flooded out people who got here by boat!
Had Trump Been Captain of HMS Titanic
Attention! All First Class passengers must board life boats on top deck! Second and Third Class Steerage passengers are directed to lower G Deck for a fantastic late nite concert by the Hartley Band
TITANIC

Trump Pops Into 18-Wheeler Truck On White House South Lawn Honking The Horn March 23, 2017 While His Health Bill Was Dying In Congress

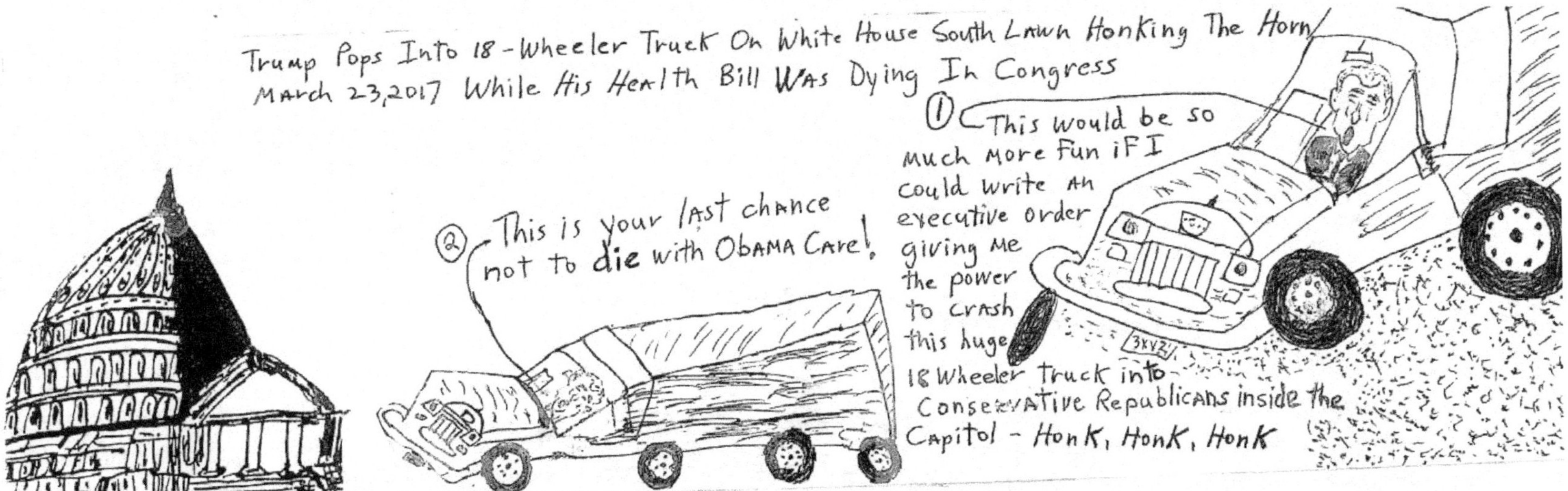

Rep. Trey Gowdy Uses His Time At Russian Hearing To Question FBI Director On White House Leaks 3/20/2017

① Is it legal for reporters to publish classified information such as Flynn's phone call which led to his resignation for lying to V.P. Pence about his talks with the Russian Ambassador over U.S. sanctions against Russia?

③ But Flynn would be here today to serve our great president, Donald J. Trump!

② No reporter has ever been prosecuted for publishing classified information during my lifetime. If Flynn's talks had not come out we might not be here today!

Kelly Anne Conway Defends Trump's Claim That Obama Wiretapped His Phone By Suggesting Even Wider Surveillance Is Possible March 13, 2017

President Trump's Budget Director Mick Mulvaney Defends The Proposed Budget Cuts To Social Programs March 16, 2017

Secretary of Health & Human Services Ton Price Spends 100s of Thousand Dollars On Private Chartered Airplane Trips Then Calls For Limo Service To Plane 9/20/17

Trump Goes After NFL Players Who Refuse To Stand For National Anthem By Kneeling Inst
Sept. 23, 2017

Trump Says Since He Became President He Has Renovated And Modernized The U.S.
Nuclear Arsenal   August 8, 2017

Treasury Secretary Steve Mnuchin's Fellow Jewish Classmates From Yale University Class oF 1985 Urge Him To Resig
From Trump Administration From Response To White Supremacy Groups By President —   August 18, 20
Mnuchin's Response

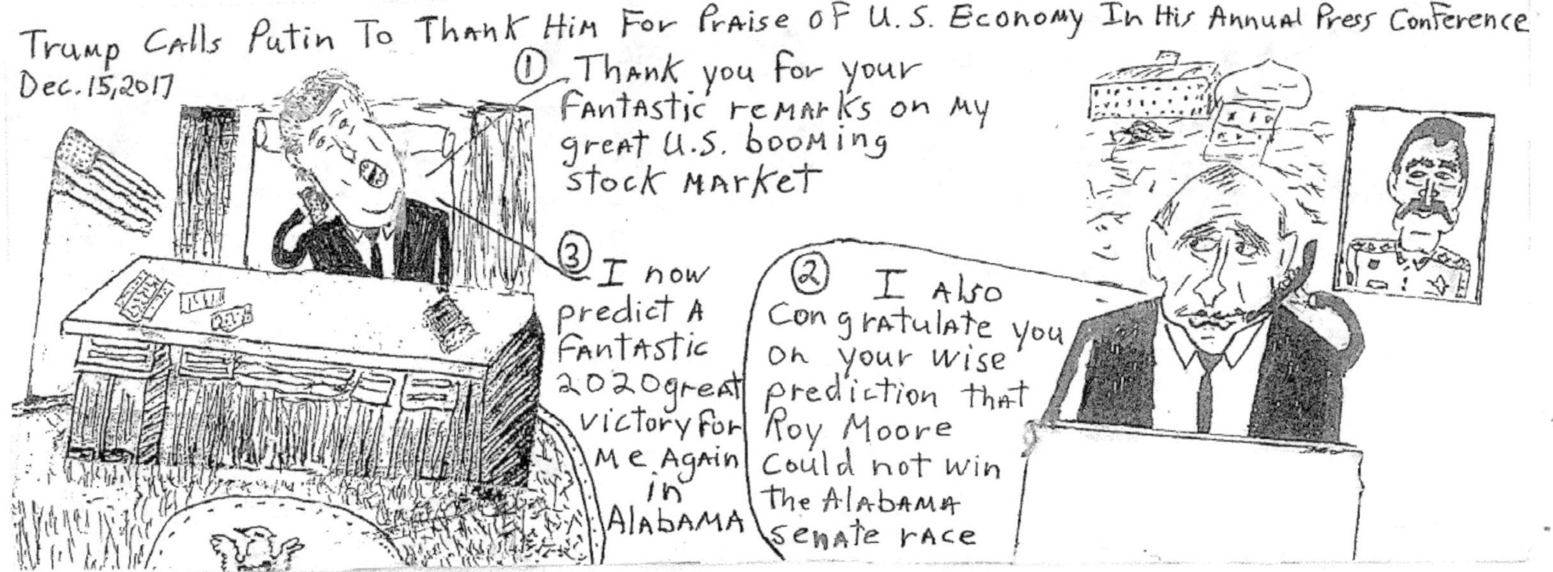

President Trump On His Telephone Conversation With Vladimir Putin Nov. 21, 2017

We talked very strongly about Syria. We talked very strongly about North Korea. We talked very strongly about Ukraine. And I strongly believe President Putin strongly believes every thing he very strongly said. We had a very good telephone conversation.

Trump Supports Roy Moore In Florida Panhandle Near The State Line With Alabama Where Moore Is Running For U.S. Senate In Special Election Dec. 8, 2017 - Trump Attacking A Moore Female Accuser On Sexual Misconduct Allegations

Sen. Lindsey Graham Says "I'd Stand Up To Trump But I'm Trying To Get Taxes Cut"

After Trump Rips Senator Corker That Corker Couldn't Get Elected Dog Catcher, Corker Tweets "Alert Day Care Staff" On Trump Oct. 24, 2017

Mike Flynn Ex-National Security Adviser Says He Agreed To Plead Guilty And Testify Against Trump For Family And Country Dec. 1, 2017

Trump On His Voting Commission Asking States To Hand Over Confidential Voter Data
June 30, 2017

Trump Fires Anthony Scaramucci, WH Communications Director As — John Kelly Takes Over As White House Chief Of Staff In A Below Gone With The Wind → Like Scene July 31, 2017

Trump Says He Has An "Absolute Right" To Control The Justice Department Dec. 28, 2017

I have stayed uninvolved with the Justice Department for purposes of hopefully thinking I'M going to be treated Fairly. We will see what happens if I'M not treated Fairly...

©2018 Richard Friedman

Trump Visits Long Island To Continue Fight Against MS-13 Gang In Speech To Suffolk County Police
July 28, 2017

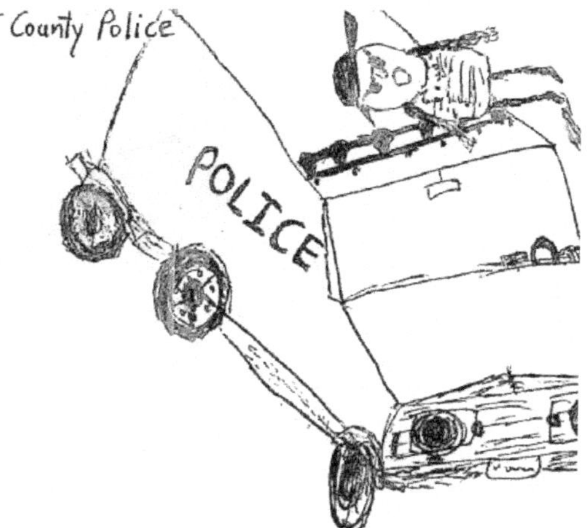

— When I see you guys putting
somebody in the car and you're
protecting their head, the way
you put the hand over, like —
Don't hit their head! I say you
can take the hand away, OK!
Here's officer Joe "Mad Dog" McGoon
who fractured 5 skulls in his
police cruiser last month.

Anthony Scaramucci During His Brief White House Tenure Tells A Journalist That He Wasn't Like Steve Bannon In A Crude Way - July 27, 2017 - As He <u>Just Imagines</u> Steve Bannon

President Trump's Fantasy Sign After Raging At His Attorney General Jeff Sessions Over His Recusal From Russia Investigation July 19, 2017   ©2018 Richard Friedman

Trump Defends His First Response To Violence In Charlottesville Blaming Both Sides In News Conference At Trump Tower August 16, 2017

© 2018 Richard Friedman

IF Ghost of Walter Cronkite Returned to The Oval Office To Report On Trump's Media Attack
Feb. 17, 2017

I'll say it to you....
Mister Unbelievable —
outlets such as the
New York Times, CNN, ABC,
NBC, And your CBS Are
not my enemy but the
enemy of the American
People. The only exception
is FOX News. They've
been really great to Me,
MOST OF The Time.

And that's
the WAY it is...
And that's the
WAY it is.

IF FormerFirst Lady Barbara Bush Visited Pres. Trump After His Inauguration In Jan., 2017

Newt Gingrich Says President Trump Is Being Attacked By the Spear Of The Deep State   August 3, 2017

3. The Baking of President Trump's
Victory of 2016
      The Democrat Candidates

Bernie Sanders Says He Was Born In New York
I was born in New York City. Political Revolution is in my New York blood.
A Future To Believe In
©2018 Richard Friedman
Bernie Sanders Defends Hillary Clinton At The Democratic Debate In Las Vegas Oct. 13, 2015
This may not be great politics but the American people are sick and tired about hearing about your damn e-mails!
Me too HA HA!
That's it! When I'm President in 2017 Bernie will be my FBI boss!
©2018 Richard Friedman
Sanders Debates Donald Trump
— I have the fantastic support of 99% of all the White Supremacist Groups. There's one of my Skin Heads!
TRUMP
White Power
— Look! I have the support of 100% of all the Jewish Guilt Groups. Here's one of my Sons of Sigmund!
A Future To Believe In
©2018 Richard Friedman

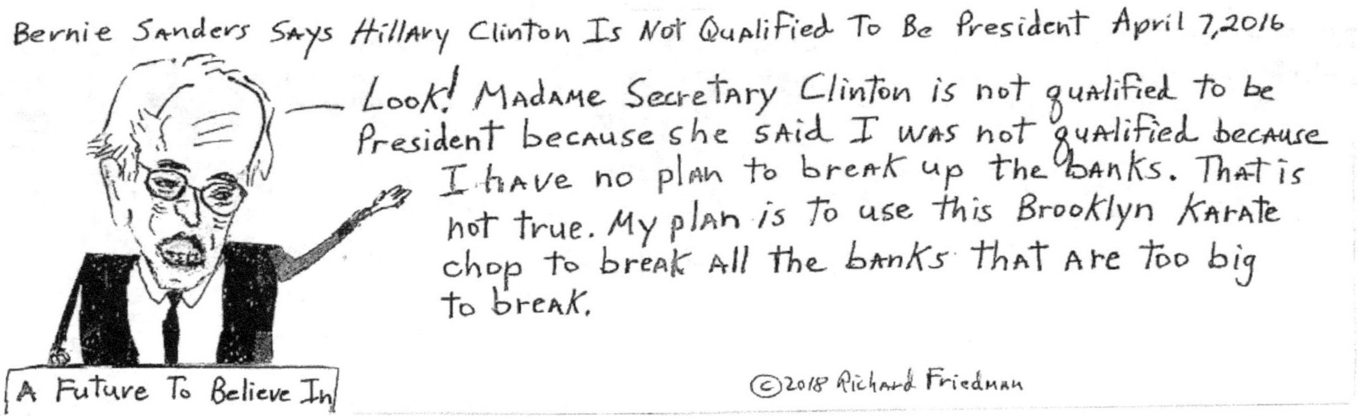

Bernie Sanders Says Hillary Clinton Is Not Qualified To Be President April 7, 2016

Look! Madame Secretary Clinton is not qualified to be President because she said I was not qualified because I have no plan to break up the banks. That is not true. My plan is to use this Brooklyn karate chop to break all the banks that are too big to break.

A Future To Believe In

©2018 Richard Friedman

Hillary Clinton Says Former Sec. of State Colin Powell Advised Her To Use A Private E-MAIL Server Aug. 21, 2016

② She was using her private e-mail server well before I sent her a memo telling her I used my private e-mail to convey Saddam's only weapon of mass destruction was now only horse shit.

① He made me do it!

©2018 Richard Friedman

Pope Francis Says He Will Not Meet Bernie Sanders At Vatican April 14, 2016

Bernie if you are elected president when you die you will be canonized as Saint Bernie for this miracle.

©2018 Richard Friedman

I want the Pope to know that I will be elected president. And that I can not be canonized because I'm allergic to gun powder.

Hillary Clinton Says "I May Have Short-Circuited The Truth" When She Claimed FBI Director James Comey Said She Was "truthful" About Her Private EMAILS Aug. 5, 2016

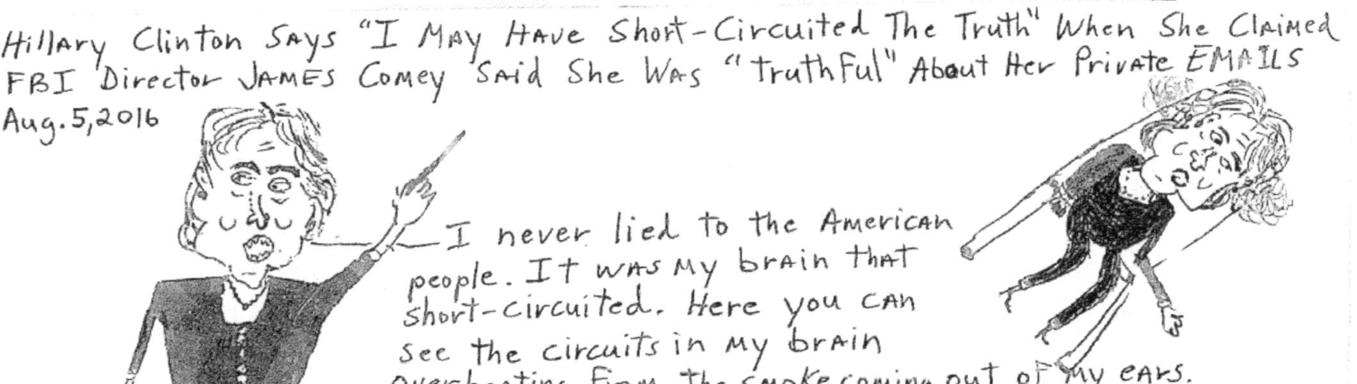

A Veteran Waiting 6 Months For His Enlarged Prostate Operation Responds After Hillary Says Veterans AFFairs Scandal Is Not Widespread   October 23, 2015

Bernie Sanders Plan For Defeating ISIS January 11, 2016

Hillary Clinton Says "I May Have Short-Circuited The Truth" When She Claimed FBI Director James Comey Said She Was "truthful" About Her Private EMAILS Aug. 5, 2016

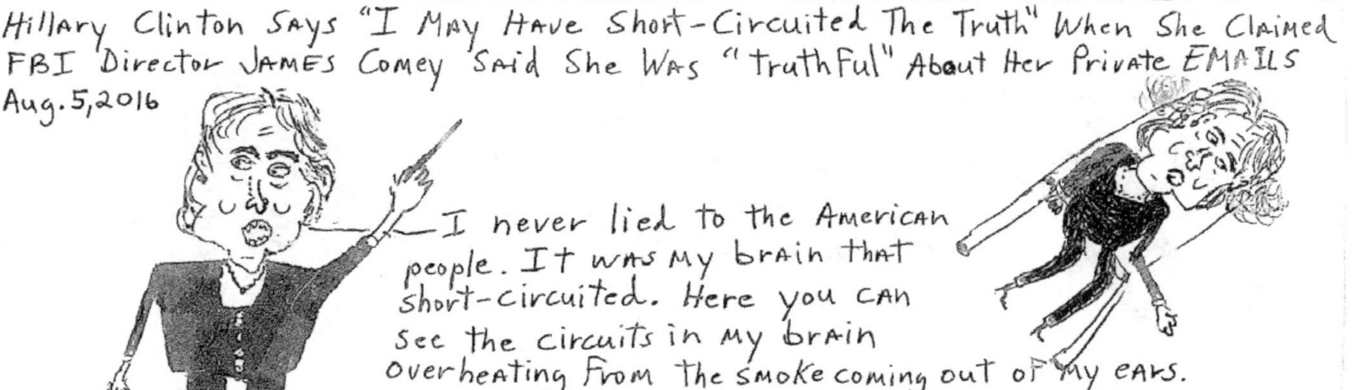

A Veteran Waiting 6 Months For His Enlarged Prostate Operation Responds After Hillary Says Veterans Affairs Scandal Is Not Widespread   October 23, 2015

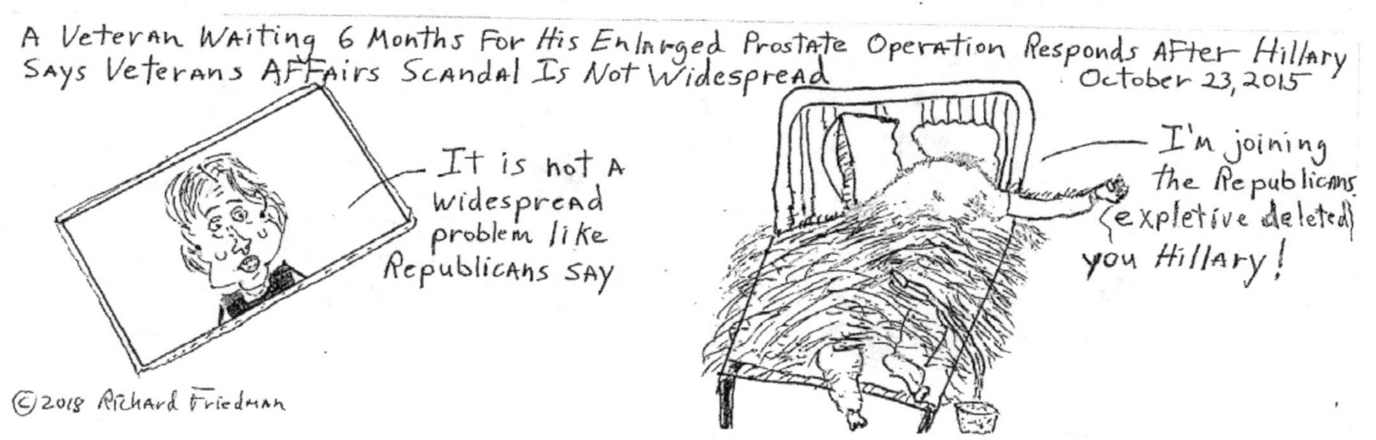

Bernie Sanders Says Terrorism Is Caused By Climate Change Nov. 16, 2015
The number one cause of terrorism is that the world is getting warmer. To cool things off when I am elected President to the terrorist hot spots I will send these Anti-Terror Windmills.
© 2018 Richard Friedman

Hillary Clinton Says She Will Put Bill In Charge Of The Economy May 16, 2016
② I predict a big bust in the economy that will be felt
① I will put my husband here in charge of the economy just because he knows what he is doing!
© 2018 Richard Friedman

Feb. 29, 2016 Hillary Clinton Goes On The Attack Against Trump   © 2018 Richard Friedman
Donald Trump builds walls I build bridges
Welcome All To The Hillary Clinton BRIDGE

Hillary Clinton Defends Her Ties To Uranium One Company That Was Granted Permission To Sell Out To Russians After Its Chairman Donated 2.3 Million To the Clinton Foundation While She Was Secretary Of State

- There is not a shred of evidence that as Secretary of State I took actions to support any donors. If I had known this was going to come up I would not have shredded all my E-MAILS. I will admit my Reset Button with President Putin did not work too good. Let's try it on IRAN.

©2018 Richard Friedman

Bernie Sanders Stays In Race As Hillary Clinton's Shield Against TRUMP March 16, 2016

©2018 Richard Friedman

TRUMP

IRF, IRF, IRFF

CLINTON

Bernie Sanders

Bernie Sanders Heads North To ALASKA March 26, 2016

©2018 Richard Friedman

When I'm President you all will live in An Igloo like this

A Future To Believe In

Hillary Clinton When Asked About Her Enemies At The Democrat Debate October 13, 2015

Bernie Sanders Goes After The Black Vote In Flint, Michigan Debate With Hillary

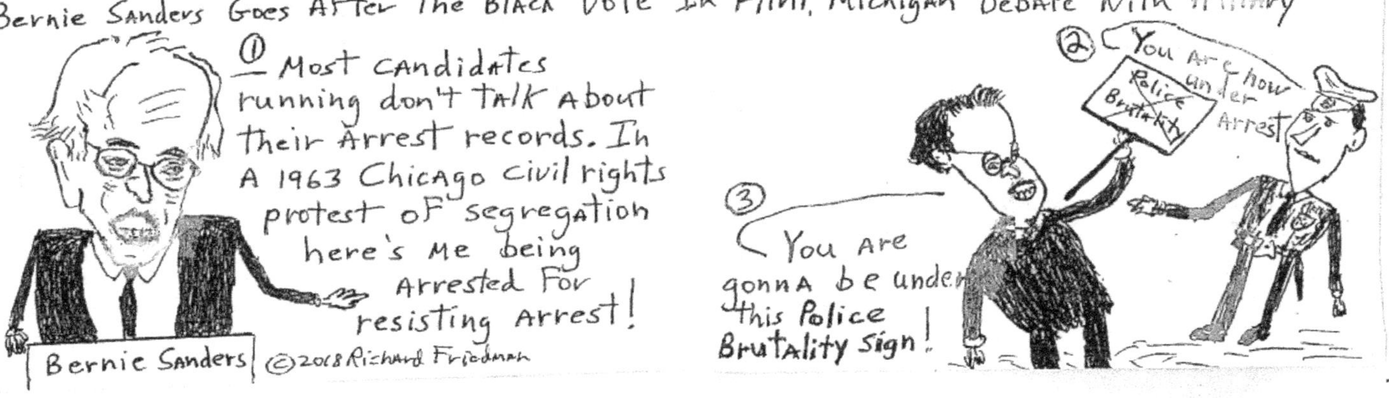

Hillary Clinton's Defense For The Benghazi, Libya Terrorist Attack of Sept. 11, 2012 Before The Benghazi Select Committee On Oct. 22, 2015   ©2018 Richard Friedman

—When Ambassador Stevens who was killed in the Attack joked about picking up "Fire sale items" From the Brits, which were security barricades that the British were no longer using because the danger in Benghazi prompted them to leave, I thought it showed their entrepreneurial spirit. Ambassador Stevens never indicated to me there was A security problem. Our diplomatic security professionals are excellent people And highly competent. I take responsibility For what happened in Benghazi. STRONGER TOGETHER we must MOVE On!

STRONGER TOGETHER

Illary Clinton On Enforcing Federal Anti-Drug Laws On States Legalizing Marijuana
c.21, 2015

The Future IF Hillary Clinton Elected In 2016 On Her First Day In Office As U.S. President

Today... My First executive order is that all Presidential emails can only be marked classified by the President of the United States. Any Republicans who want my personal e-mail server can check it out in the Men's room of Popeyes Chicken located at 4309 Wisconsin Ave. Washington, D.C.

Have a good lunch! © 2018 Richard Friedman

3. The Baking of President Trump's
   Victory of 2016
      The Republican Candidates

Trump Hits Clinton Over Her Top Aide's Husband Sexting Scandal August 29, 2016

Kasich Says He Will Drop Out of The Race After Trump Wins Indiana On May 3, 2016
And Calls Him A Disgusting And Sloppy Eater

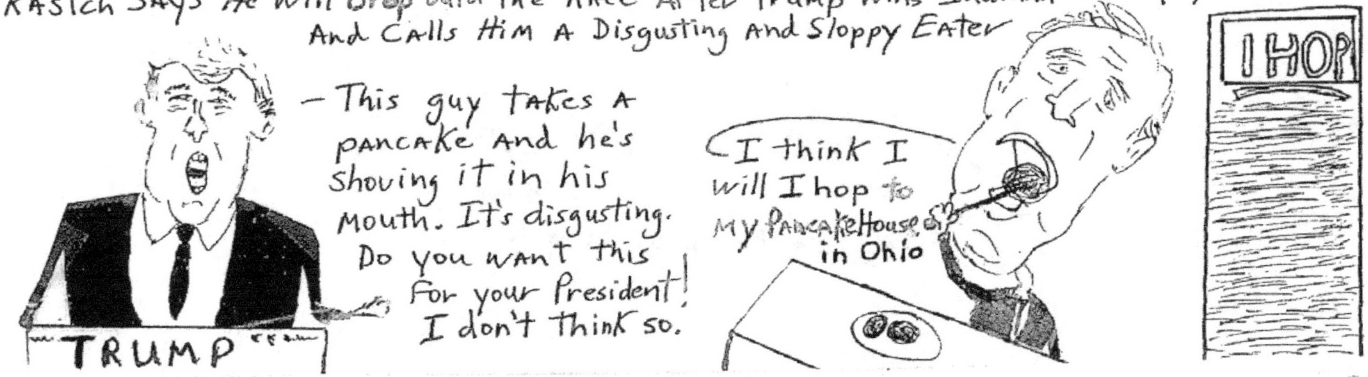

Huckabee Enters The Presidential Race For 2016   Feb. 2, 2015

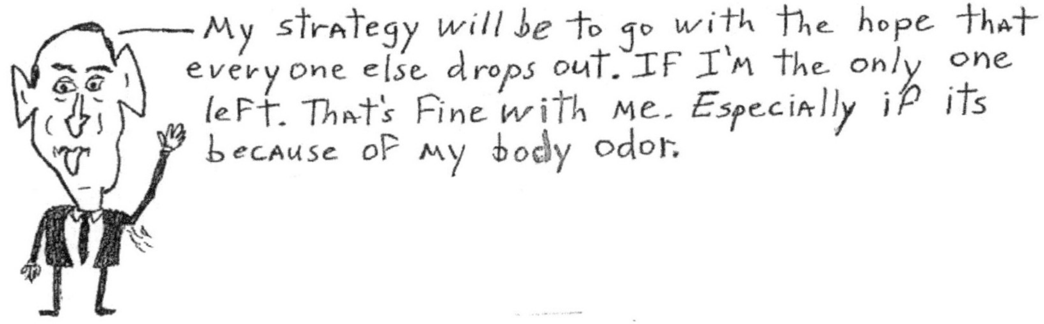

Donald Trump Vows To Make Mexico Pay For Border Wall IF Elected

Ben Carson Confesses To A Big Sin He Left Out Of His Book November 6, 2015

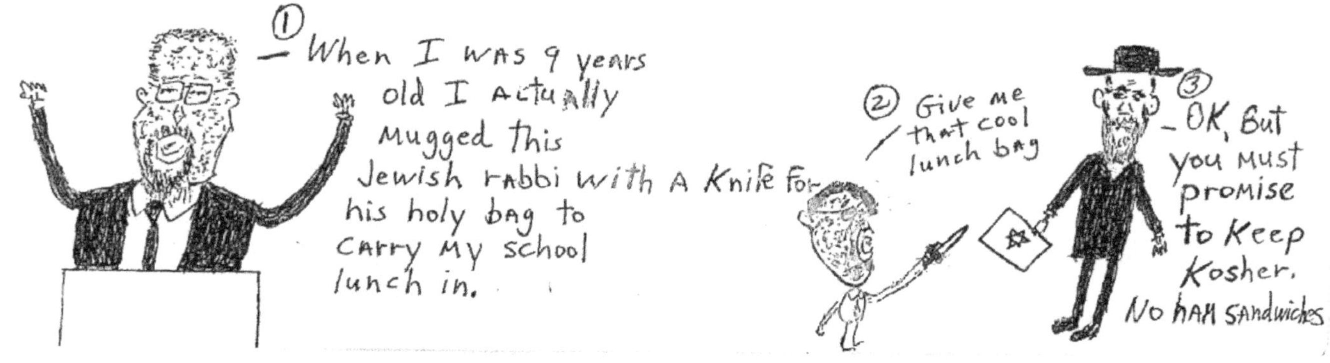

Jeb Bush Posts Video Featuring His Mother Endorsing His Campaign Jan. 19, 2016

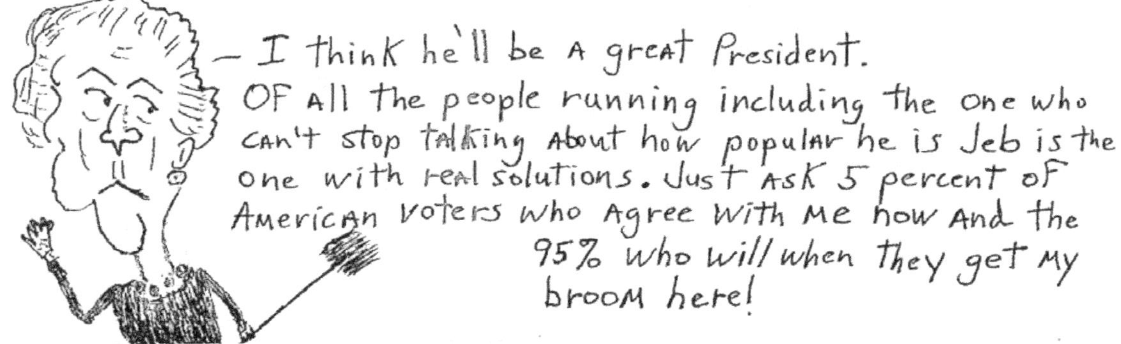

The Latest Attack Ad Against Donald Trump From Chinese Lady Who Worked At His Mar-a-Lago Estate In Palm Beach, Florida

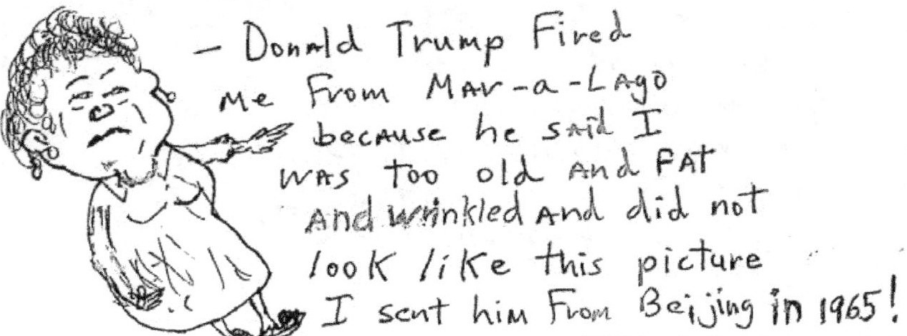

Former President George W. Bush On Brother Jeb Running In 2016

Sen. Ted Cruz At The Republican Debate Implies He Would Nuke Iran Over 10 U.S. Sailors Seized In Iranian Waters January 14, 2016

— Any country that makes U.S. service members get on their knees will feel the Full Force and Fury of the great United States of America when I am President.

Look, we nuked Japan for sinking a few battleships...
Same thing!

Mrs. Bush On Jeb Running For President Of The United States

Ted Cruz Says Only Good Things About Sarah Palin After She Endorses Donald Trump
Jan. 19, 2016

Trump Says Ben Carson Makes Jeb Bush Look Like ——— The 'Energizer Bunny'

September 10, 2015

Sen. Lindsey Graham Says Republican Party Will Face Extinction If Either Trump Or Cruz Is The Nominee For President Jan 22, 2016
With Trump or Cruz the Republican party faces extinction like the African Wild Ass Equus donkey here which became extinct during Roman Times.
That's it for me! I've had it with wild Ass donkeys! Bye!
Trump Expresses Regret For Saying The Wrong Thing August 19, 2016
Sometimes... you don't choose the right words or you say the wrong thing. I have done that. And believe it or not, I regret it. Too much is at stake for us to be consumed with these Issues. That reminds me... has anyone here tried Any of these new Fantastically delicious juicy Trump steaks?
TRUMP
Jeb Bush Answers Question On Whether His Campaign Is On Life Support October 30, 2015
It's not on life support. We have the most money. Here's my new campaign limousine!
Jeb Can Fix IT

NJ Governor Chris Christie Says Marco Rubio Is The Boy In The Bubble Who Can Only Listen To His Advisers Who Write Speeches For Him Feb. 2, 2016

Ted Cruz Slams Donald Trump Over Latest Attack From Him On His Wife March 24, 2016

Donald Trump On His Trump University Being Called Fake University

Jeb Bush Answers Donald Trump's Charge His Brother Failed To Keep Us Safe... What He Could Have Said October 19, 2015

Governor John Kasich Of Ohio On Calls From Trump + Cruz For Him To Withdraw

Trump Considers Giuliani To Lead Muslim Commission On Their Immigration May 11, 2016

Donald Trump Calls Marco Rubio Weak On Immigration November 12, 2015

Ted Cruz Issues Warning of Superbowl Electromagnetic Pulse Attack From North Korea Launched Satellite Feb. 9, 2016

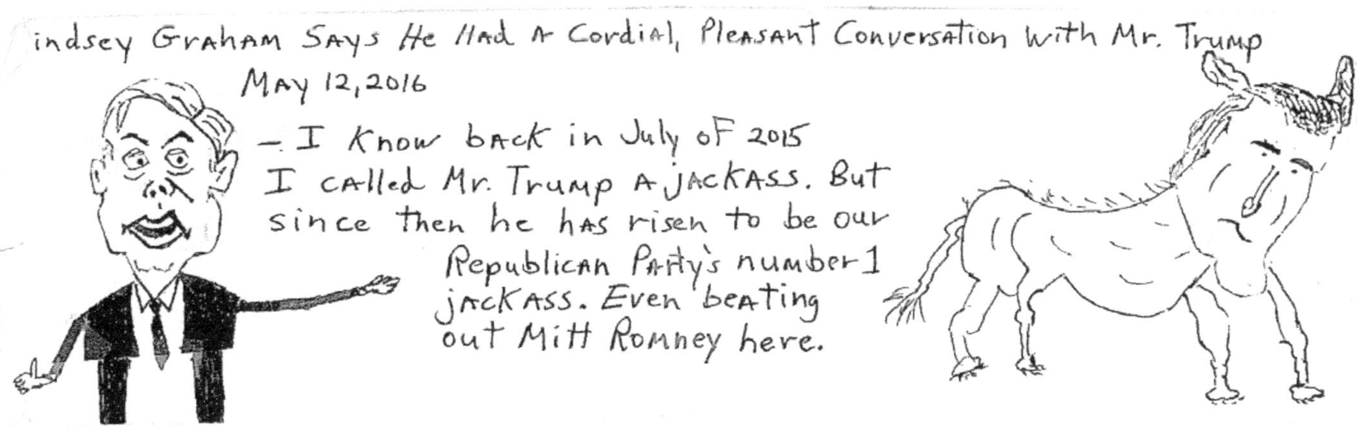

Donald Trump Calls Marco Rubio Weak On Immigration November 12, 2015

Ted Cruz Issues Warning of Superbowl Electromagnetic Pulse Attack From North Korea Launched Satellite Feb. 9, 2016

indsey Graham Says He Had A Cordial, Pleasant Conversation with Mr. Trump May 12, 2016

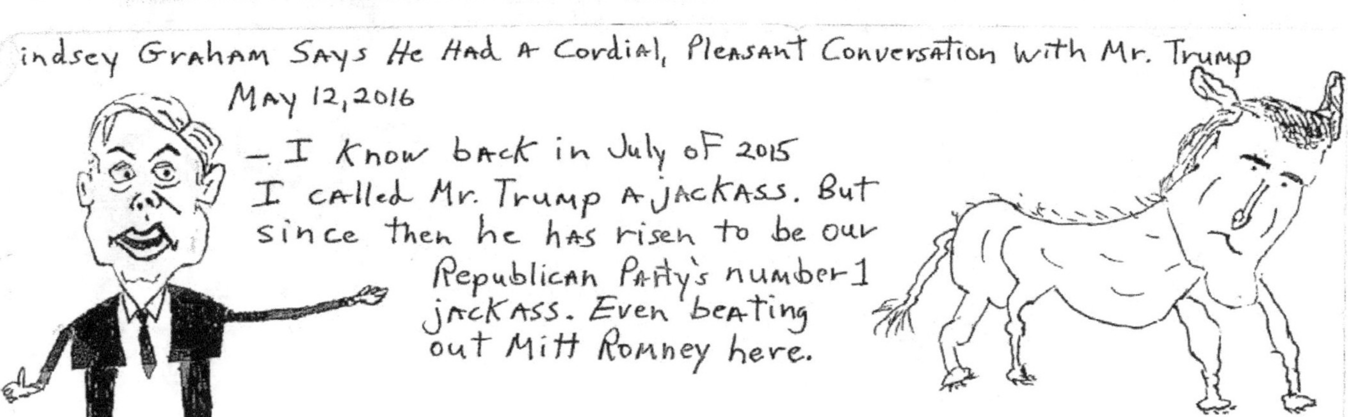

Ted Cruz Drops Out oF the Presidential Race AFter Losing Indiana And Asks God For Forgiveness May 4, 2016 Day After And Then Hears A Response From The Lord

Gov. Chris Christie Threatens Ted Cruz AFter Cruz Fails To Endorse Trump At The Republican Convention In Ohio July 20, 2016

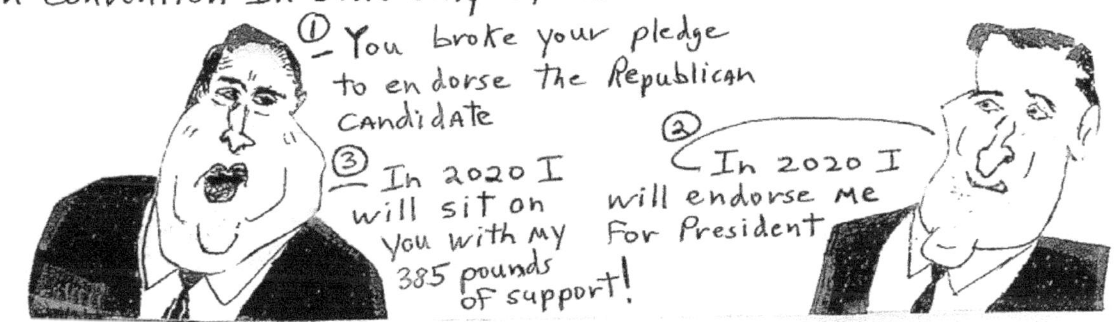

When Rick Perry Is Elected He Keeps His Campaign Promise To Rip Up The Iranian Nuke Deal On His First Day In OFFice

Lincoln's Gettysburg Address Nov. 19, 1863 Compared To Trump's Gettysburg Oct. 22, 2016

Trump ConFuses 9/11 with 7-Eleven At Buffalo Rally April 19, 2016